·WANNABE·

A Would-Be Player's Misadventures in Hollywood

EVERETT WEINBERGER

A Buzz Book

St. Martin's Press ≈ New York

Web Site: http://www.buzzmag.com

Library of Congress Cataloging-in-Publication Data

Weinberger, Everett.
    Wannabe : a would-be player's misadventures in Hollywood
/ Everett Weinberger.
       p.   cm.
    Originally published: New York : Carol Pub. Group, c1995.
    ISBN 0-312-15708-8
    1. Motion picture industry—California—Los Angeles—
Anecdotes. I. Title.
PN1993.5.U65W36   1997
384'.8'0979494—dc21   97-16873
                                      CIP

First published in the United States of America by A Birch Lane
Press Book, a division of the Carol Publishing Group

First Buzz Book Edition: September 1997

10 9 8 7 6 5 4 3 2 1

To my parents for their love and support,
and for inspiring me in very different ways.

Nil desperandum, wannabeus

CONTENTS

PREFACE

wan|na·be (wän'ə bē', wô'-) **n.** [Slang] a person who wants to be or be like someone else or to attain some status or condition /a rockstar *wannabe*/: also **wan'|na-be'**

Webster's New World Dictionary,
Third College Edition

Nowhere is the word "wannabe" more prevalent than in Hollywood, where everyone seems to want to exchange his position for another, and where raw desire is as admired and as much on display as the Porsches that ply the city's freeways. I admit it: I was a wannabe movie producer five years ago. Like a modern-day Sammy Glick, I wanted to make it so badly, I would have done almost anything for anyone. And yet the more I hungered, the more remote my chances for success became. The smell of desperation is not a marketable scent, especially in Hollywood.

I was also a young man in a hurry. But at twenty-six, one tends to believe that a year is a millennium and that a false turn is tantamount to career suicide. When I read my account now, I know I suffer sometimes from overearnestness and even a touch of sanctimony. But these were my feelings at the time *in extremis*. I must also emphasize that this was my account alone: It need not be everyone's experience.

This book has its genesis in the diary I kept, initially as a way of recording my progress, and eventually as a cathartic means of preserving my sanity. I soon realized that my experiences could serve as a guide book of sorts for others who I know are out there, dreaming of altering their life course and catching the next flight to L.A. It is the kind of book I would have appreciated reading before starting out. Not that someone else's account would have stopped me—I was too cocky. But it might have toughened me for what was to come.

Have things changed in five years? Unequivocally, no. If anything, tougher times and leaner budgets in Hollywood have made prospects for hopefuls bleaker still. This is a tough, unforgiving business, as the Japanese are learning. And who are bigger wannabes than corporations like Matsushita and Sony, who have poured billions into the industry in pursuit of illusive synergies? They, along with Turner, PolyGram, Samsung, and other wannabe moguls, are invaluable to the system, for they supply the cash flow needed to maintain the status quo in Hollywood and thus ensure its continuity. The players change but the game stays the same.

Getting this book published was itself a long road. I think I first believed in it when I phoned a literary agent in Beverly Hills after sending her a copy of the manuscript. She berated me for fifteen minutes. I knew I was on to something if a member of the Hollywood establishment would get *that* upset.

The experiences in this book all took place, though for the sake of the narrative, I made slight changes to the chronology of events. (As I soon realized, while movies proceed in some comprehensible sequence, real life unfortunately does not.) Where it seemed appropriate to protect the privacy of certain friends, coworkers, and fellow wannabes, I have fictionalized names and changed identities. All other names and events are factual.

ACKNOWLEDGMENTS

I owe much thanks to my agent, B.J. Robbins, for "getting it" and for believing in the book and its premise. She was also wise enough to guide the manuscript to Kevin McDonough of Carol Publishing, who proved to be an excellent and creative editor. My thanks also at Carol to Kent Holland for his tireless promotion, and India Cooper for her inspired copyediting.

Linda Keslar deserves my gratitude for her friendship in my time of need, and for introducing me to B.J. Special thanks to Howard Altmann, Victor Harary, and Valerie Hood for their insightful criticism on early drafts. Also thanks to Pam Brewster, Cal Cooper, Michael Lustig, William Passmore, Sarah Ross, Mitch Rubin, and Jeff Wolf for their helpful comments. And finally, for their friendship, support, and encouragement (and because who knows when I'll have this opportunity again), my brother, Teddy, and my sisters, Jessica and Marissa, Alexandra Aleskovsky, Margaret Chu, Aaron Freilich, Daniel Geber, Mike Gold of Beyond Fitness, Scott Kapchan, Joey Matalon, Jeremy Rees, Mason Sleeper, Kevin Toner, Wayne Weddington, and Rick Wolf.

·WANNABE·

CHAPTER 1

Me, Alec, and Kim

Fame is vapor; popularity an accident; the only earthly certainty is oblivion.

MARK TWAIN

Alec Baldwin wheezed and coughed. He was lying down on the black leather couch in Kim Basinger's production office in Beverly Hills as I walked in for my interview. Hollywood's premier leading man blew his nose and looked miserable. He leaned slightly upright and weakly shook my hand.

"I got this cold in New York," he said in a husky voice, sniffling to accentuate. "Happens when I fly back and forth too quickly."

"Yeah, I know what you mean," I said. "A quick shift in weather can do that to you."

"Hold on a sec..." He leaned his head back and squeezed eye drops into his sky-blue eyes.

He squinted while he studied my resumé, trying to think of a good interview question. I, in turn, scrutinized Baldwin. This unkempt but handsome thirty-two-year-old actor, after all, was one of the top three male draws in the movies in the fall of 1990, following the recent success of *The Hunt for Red October*, which had grossed over $120 million. After his supporting roles in *Beetlejuice, Married to the Mob, Working Girl*, and *Talk Radio, The Hunt* was Baldwin's breakthrough film. It was to be the first of three Tom Clancy novels headed for production with Alec Baldwin starring as CIA analyst Dr. Jack Ryan.

"What is this student investment club?" he finally asked. I couldn't believe that of all the items on my resumé, he was asking about an insignificant college club.

"It was a student-run fund I helped form that raised money from students and invested in the stock market."

"Um, hmm." He put my resumé down. "Everett, do you know what's really involved in being my personal assistant?"

"Yeah, I think I understand the gist of it." I really had no clue about what the position entailed, but I knew it was just this sort of job that launched people's careers in Hollywood. Hadn't *Die Hard* producer Joel Silver gotten his start as producer Larry Gordon's driver?

"Well, I'm not sure you know what you're in for. I need a right-hand man—someone I can count on, no matter what it is. Someone who's going to travel with me everywhere I go. *Everywhere*—no matter where or when. You'll go first class all the way, but you gotta be willing to move within a minute's notice."

That sounds *so* bad: eating hors d'oeuvres in first class with Alec, fighting off beautiful groupies at airports, sleeping in five-star hotels.

"No problem, that's exactly what I expect. Listen, I'm single, I have no pets, and I can pack up in five minutes. Plus, I have nothing against first-class travel."

He laughed, and I beamed back. "Okay, but you also have to be willing to run errands like picking up my dry cleaning or going to the store and buying things for me. All the typical personal assistant stuff. Now, as a Stanford MBA—the truth—are you *really* ready for that part of the job too?"

Here was where I had to sell myself. "Actually, I think that will be the easy part of the job for me, Alec. You see, I'm *very* efficient, and I can run your errands more quickly and better than anyone else can. I'll then have time to do more of the other, more complicated things." Whatever those might be.

"That's good, because I also need someone to run my office—take charge of it, computerize all the files, floppy disks, software, hardware, and everything else on the computer." I could tell right away that Baldwin was not exactly a computer scientist.

"I'm an expert on both PCs and Macintoshes. I also know almost every major software program, and if I don't know it, I can quickly learn it."

He ran his hand through his jet-black hair, leaned over, and stared at me. "The point is, Everett, I don't deal with a lot of people. Besides my family, I deal with my agent, my manager, my assistant, and Kim, of course." Kim Basinger and Baldwin were Hollywood's couple of the moment, photographed in all the right places in New York and Los Angeles.

He brought his hands together and formed a circle. "It's like concentric circles around me. I get bombarded with calls and letters each day. You have no idea. You've got to deal with whatever or whoever comes in, and sift through it so I don't have to spend all my day dealing with crap."

Oh please, Alec, please let me deal with your crap. Okay, swallow your pride. "Alec," I said, pointing my finger at him and pausing for effect. "I can run your office, and your life, better than anyone you've ever had or ever will, without a doubt."

He smiled. He liked that super-confidence bit.

I decided to take the initiative. "Can I ask you something important? Have you actually fired your current assistant yet?"

He looked embarrassed. "N-no...not just yet. I want to have someone in place before I do that. It's a very delicate situation—trust me. You know, this guy worked for Stallone before me." He seemed impressed that he had scored Rocky Balboa's assistant. Was he scared that if he fired him, Stallone would come by and beat the daylights out of him? I was nervous about getting my hopes up for nothing.

I had been placed in this unlikely position by a phone call I had received the week before from Nick Styne, who worked at Mighty Wind Productions, Kim Basinger's production company. He told me they were interviewing candidates for Alec Baldwin and I had been recommended by one of the many production executives I met during the past six months of my job search in Los Angeles.

I drove to Basinger's offices the next day, trying to position in my mind the answer to the inevitable question of why in God's name a business type like me would want to be Alec Baldwin's personal slave. I would need to emphasize the access to power brokers and the opportunities that could arise. Flattery would definitely come in handy. At the very least, I figured it would make a good story for my sisters.

Lost in thought, I suddenly jolted to a stop on Santa Monica Boulevard. I had nearly run over an old woman wearing a tattered red raincoat who was slowly shuffling across the street hunched over a shopping cart. I hated these crosswalks in L.A.

I maneuvered into a spot in the basement parking lot of a three-story glass building on North Maple Drive in a residential section of Beverly Hills. I pocketed the parking ticket, hoping they'd at least validate for the parking fee. I was ten minutes early and, as usual, headed straight for the men's room and my pre-interview routine. Peering intently at myself in the mirror, I brushed my hand over my hair a few times, straightened my tie, and splashed water on my face.

"Hi there! Hey, Alec! Nice to meet you. Hi!" I practiced smiling a few times until I didn't think I looked phony anymore. I was ready to be everything they wanted in a personal assistant.

Nick Styne was the first person I met at Mighty Wind Productions. As far as I could see, he functioned as receptionist, secretary, computer programmer, script reader, and gofer. He was a tall, blue-eyed California blonde wearing jeans, a navy blazer, and a white T-shirt, and looked like an ad for lite beer. I felt like a geek in my ex–investment banker suit. I sat in the waiting area and chatted with him while playing with a toy slot machine they had on the front table. After fifteen minutes of requisite waiting, I was introduced to Barbara Dreyfus, Kim Basinger's director of development, in charge of ferreting out worthwhile film projects for the actress.

She shook my hand firmly. "Pleased to meet you." Barbara was a slim brunette in her early thirties with a low, throaty voice that betrayed her New York upbringing. She was dressed in a strapless black party dress with a slit that ran all the way up to her behind, de rigueur dress code, I supposed, for Kim Basinger's office.

"So, you met Nick?"

"Yeah, nice guy."

"I don't know if you know, but he's also Jule Styne's son...You know, *Jule Styne*, the famous Broadway songwriter?"

"Really? Wow!" What else was I supposed to say: Oh yeah, well, I'm the son of Leonard Weinberger...You know—the lawyer from Queens?

She pinched her lips and looked at me for a minute. "Do you know what this position demands? I don't think you do. Twenty-four, seven, fifty-two." She paused, and I thought she was testing my arithmetic capabilities. "This job is twenty-four hours a day, seven days a week, fifty-two weeks a year. It demands total dedication. It's exactly what I give to Kim day in and day out...Actually, Alec wants someone exactly like me. But Alec can't have me." She lingered over the man's name as if it were a benediction: Aaaa-lekk, Aaaa-lekk.

"So Alec wants a clone of me, someone to take control of his life. Alec is the hottest commodity in Hollywood, and everyone wants a piece of him—*everyone*. You have to be able to take an assignment and give Alec the confidence that you can handle it. Period. No bullshit. No fuss. It's done." She snapped her fingers.

I watched her as she got out of her chair and walked to the window. She was on a roll, and I had no intention of interrupting her. Development executives feel absolutely confident about very few topics, and this was obviously one for Barbara. She came back to the front of the desk, sat on top with her long legs crossed, and peered down at me.

"Why do you want this position? And I must say, that's really a rhetorical question, because I think this is the hottest job in town."

"I don't want to be a personal assistant for ten years. Ultimately, I want to be a movie producer. And I think—and correct me if I'm wrong—that working for Alec would provide me with the exposure and contacts needed to make that happen. I think it's probably one of the best vantage points I could have in the business."

"You're damn right it is." She was already selling me on the job—definitely a good sign. "Alec can snap his fingers and overnight make you a producer on one of his films. Right now, I would say without a doubt that Alec and Kim are the hottest two actors in town."

She glanced at my resumé for a few seconds. "I see you studied political science at Columbia. That's good, *very* good. I don't know if you know, but Alec also studied political science in college." I did know this from my research. After growing up in suburban Long Island, Baldwin had attended George Washington and had transferred to NYU to study acting, though he left school a few credits short of his bachelor's degree. "He's very politically involved and has major political ambitions." I raised my eyebrows involuntarily.

"Oh yeah. He's totally committed to public service, and he's got everything going for him: looks, brains, drive. Trust me, the man will be a senator one day." She paused and looked at me conspiratorially. "That doesn't leave this room," she said, as if she had imparted a major national secret.

"Really? That's interesting—I didn't know that." I nodded, trying to show that I was impressed, but inwardly I was laughing at the prospect of this former soap opera star in Congress. Still, stranger things have happened. Wasn't Clint Eastwood once mayor of Carmel, Sonny Bono mayor of Palm Springs, and Gopher of *The Love Boat* a U.S. congressman?

She peered at me for what seemed like minutes. I peered back until her head seemed twice as large as her body.

"You have very nice blue eyes, you know that?"

"Th-thanks..." Not your standard interview fare.

"Okay, I'm going to give you a little quiz question that I've asked all the candidates." Now this was unorthodox. Still, I felt confident I could handle anything she'd throw at me. Go ahead, babe, ask me my strengths and weaknesses.

She put her two index fingers on her lips, contemplating the right phrasing for this all-important question. "Okay...Now let's say you're on the phone with the reservations person at a very, very fancy, exclusive five-star hotel, which Alec has expressly asked you to find a room in. *But*—here's the catch—the reservations person tells you that they have no available rooms. None—no way, no how. Period." Her favorite punctuation mark. "*What* do you do?"

"I guess I'd ask to speak with the manager," I said instinctively.

She stared at me again, and I worried that I had somehow misunderstood the question. "Thank you." She extended her hand. "Thank you very, very much. I just want you to know that you're the first person we've seen to answer that question correctly. The first one. Finally." She called Nick Styne in to tell him my brilliant answer.

"Stop," I said, laughing. "You're embarrassing me." My face turned red, as I disliked undeserved praise. "I can't believe no one else said that—it's kind of intuitive." I wanted to ask her what kind of dim bulbs she had seen before me, but refrained.

She stood up as if to conclude our chat. I couldn't believe that constituted an interview. She squeezed my arm as she led me out of the office and let me know that I was one of two people she would recommend to meet Alec. I had been granted the right to see the wizard himself. As I walked down the hall, I began whistling "Follow the Yellow Brick Road."

Now, a week later, I had finished my meeting with the wizard and was walking out of the office when Barbara rushed at me. "Oh Everett, do you have a sec?"

I turned around and was face to face with Kim Basinger. I was surprised by how much shorter she was up close than I had imagined. I'm only five-eight but was taller than she. Though clad in faded jeans and an old denim shirt, the thirty-six-year-old movie star was still beautiful. My eyes remained locked on hers as Barbara continued: "Kim would like to talk with you for a few minutes—if you have the time, that is . . ." Barbara did seem to be smirking when she said this. Yeah, like I don't have time for the sexiest woman on earth. I just hoped my mouth wasn't hanging open. I followed Basinger to her office, feeling like a monkey in the zoo at feeding time.

She began a disjointed monologue in her soft, southern voice. "My life with Alec is complicated, *very* complicated. He's a complicated man, too. He's got all these demands on him. Everyone wants a piece of him. *Everyone*: studios, agents, producers, directors, charities, fans. He's hot right now. He's big and he's going to be bigger still. He's also very politically minded."

"Yes, Barbara told me. I think it's great that he wants to get involved." My eyes kept moving from her eyes to her perfect, glistening lips.

"He's real smart too, book and street smarts. He's *very* intelligent and needs someone just like him watching out for him." She paused. "Barbara says you're really smart. Is that true?"

Actually, Kim, I'm a total idiot. I smiled modestly. "Well, I don't want to brag, but I'm confident that I can handle anything he gives me." After all, I had passed Barbara's exam, hadn't I?

"That's good...That's exactly right...Good. 'Cause you've got to handle him, take control of his life and manage it," she said, sure that she was saying something profound. She paused and stared at me for what seemed like ages. Those juicy lips.

She wrinkled her brow. "Umm, where was I?"

"Complicated lives."

She raised her eyebrows. Was I mocking her a bit? I fought to maintain a straight face.

"Right, right. And *my* life is complicated too. Believe me. I have all these film projects, interview requests, commercials, merchandising, appearances. And we travel together constantly. I've also got this business project in Georgia." That's right, I had read about her paying $20 million in 1989 for most of the property in Braselton, Georgia, including the Bank of Braselton (Basinger was born and raised in nearby Athens). She had partnered with Ameritech Corporation, a regional phone company whose pension fund helped fund the project aimed at developing the town (population 450) into an entertainment center.

My mind began to wander. I could not believe that I was in the same room as Kim Basinger. *The* Kim Basinger of *9½ Weeks*. The guys were not going to believe this. Whether I got the job or not, I was going to have a great story.

"...and you know, we just finished a movie together for Disney. Horrible people over there. Believe me, we won't ever do a movie with them again. The bean counters there don't care a thing about art—just dollars and cents."

"Yeah, I worked there too for various executives. I know what you mean—I can sympathize. I don't think they have souls there." I wanted to egg her on. I had read all about her and Baldwin's well-publicized temper tantrums on the set of their latest film, *The Marrying Man*.

"That's exactly right. Those phone monkeys and suits don't know the first thing about making movies. All they and their executives care about is pinching pennies and following formulas." I also heard that crew members on *The Marrying Man* set had distributed T-shirts showing a red bar over a picture of a monkey talking on a cellular phone.

"You know, Alec told me he loves that you're also from New York. He thinks you'll have a strong connection with him."

I smiled, tickled by the thought of Alec Baldwin and Kim Basinger in bed at night, discussing Everett Weinberger from Brooklyn.

CHAPTER 2

The Decision

A man can stand anything except a succession of ordinary days.

JOHANN WOLFGANG VON GOETHE

Why I interviewed with Baldwin was an easy question to answer. The more difficult questions were how and why I moved to Los Angeles to break into Hollywood in the first place.

I remember where I was when I decided I had to make a drastic change in my life. It was June of 1988, several months before I was to enter the 1990 class at Stanford Business School. I was sitting in Tom Kelly's office at the investment bank in Manhattan I had joined two years prior as a financial analyst straight out of college. Kelly was one of those arrogant junior associates who cared more about the signs of Wall Street power than about love of finance. Tall and WASPy looking, with dirty blond hair slicked back, he wore gold wire-framed glasses (I was convinced they were nonprescription), a set of blue-and-red-striped suspenders, gold knotted cufflinks, monogrammed white shirt, red Hermès tie—the whole eighties package.

So I was sitting and waiting in his office, and I felt like screaming as he continued his phone conversation, showing no signs of acknowledging I was in the room. He had his chair turned to the side, and he faced the wall while squeezing a hand exerciser. I could almost understand if it had been a crucial business call, but he was discussing his golf game. I pulled my socks up, crossed my legs again, and placed my hand on his desk, wanting to play with something. I picked up a crystal paperweight from his desk and, in one of those *what if* destructive moments, thought briefly about hurling it at his head and watching the blood pour down his face. Societal norms took over, and instead I read the inscription. I found it funny that these investment banking deal mementos—delicate pieces of crystal, Tiffany clocks, or mahogany boxes—were blemished with dull financial writing engraved on them. This one read:

$75,000,000
SERIES C CONVERTIBLE EXCHANGEABLE PREFERRED STOCK
1,725,000 SHARES
ITEL CORPORATION
APRIL 16, 1987
THOMAS D. KELLY
MERRILL LYNCH CAPITAL MARKETS

I longed to leave the room and let him call me when he was ready. Why was his time more valuable than mine? But I stayed—no guts. I glanced up at him and stared. His eyes finally caught mine, and he held up his right index finger and mouthed, "One sec." I nodded and halfheartedly smiled.

"Sorry about that," he said as he put the phone down. "All right, let's see the analysis and then get Williams on the phone." He perused the spreadsheet and immediately removed a comma from one of the footnotes. He had to show me that he was in command.

He put the phone on speaker and began dialing with the eraser end of a pencil. While waiting for the client to get on the line, he leaned back in his chair, looked straight at me, and assumed the investment banker power pose: hands clasped behind his head, confidently showing no underarm stains.

"Hi, Bill," he said in his louder-than-usual power voice, "Tom Kelly at Merrill Lynch. I'm here with Elliot Weinberg." Two months on the project and the son of a bitch still couldn't say my name correctly.

"Have you seen the book we prepared?" *We* prepared? You mean *I* prepared. I was the one who stayed until three A.M. last Monday.

"Yes, Tom, I have it right in front of me." We both stared, transfixed, at the squawk box as if it were animate.

"It's just some quick and dirty analysis we've done. We ran the numbers and basically feel it's a wash between the two plans. Either one would be a total slam-dunk for the company. In a word, Bill, it's a no-brainer." That was Tom—Mr. Cliché. He never failed to throw in every investment banking platitude he could think of.

"As far as I can see," the client said, "the model makes sense although the three base cases are slightly aggressive on your growth assumptions. We were calculating internally here using a nine percent discount rate..."

As he continued droning in a low monotonous baritone, Tom pressed the mute button, a favorite trick of his. "The fucker doesn't even understand the model," he said to me conspiratorially and winked. (I was convinced that at some point during the associate training course, senior investment bankers had advised associates to use the mute button in order to foster camaraderie with analysts. They probably spent a half hour on perfecting the wink alone.) I admit that I would have been charmed by Tom's maneuvers if the guy weren't such a lout otherwise.

"Bill," Kelly said, "sorry to interrupt, but if you want us to run the numbers using more conservative assumptions, that's no problem at all. And just for shits and grins, why don't we throw in a recapitalization analysis?" He beamed and winked at me again, knowing he'd just canceled my weekend plans.

"That would be excellent, Tom. And if you could also add a stock repurchase plan as one of the options and calculate on a pro forma basis the EPS dilution of the..."

As the voice squawked on about convertible debentures and forced conversion, I looked out the window behind Kelly at the beautiful, crisp spring day. I watched a passing cruise ship, accompanied by tiny red tugboats, slowly make its way down the sun-drenched Hudson River.

I felt choked by my tight collar and tie, and as heat rushed up my neck to my face, I desperately wished I were on board the ship, sailing away from my life in New York. I knew I had to make a sharp course correction in my career path. I was already on the conveyer belt toward graduate school. The decision seemed irreversible because I didn't have the guts to turn down Stanford Business School. I was not *that* radical. I knew, however, that business school was nothing but a short-term fix. I still had to decide what the hell I was going to do for the rest of my life.

That night, back in my tiny studio apartment on the Upper West Side of Manhattan, I lay on my futon, thinking about my career options. After countless career-probing exercises, I knew my criteria for the ideal position: variety, excitement, creativity, travel, money. And I kept hearing the career advisors whispering in my ear: "Do what you love. Love what you do."

Do what you love. But what do I love? Movies. Yes, I love the movies, both film itself and all the gossip and news concerning the business and its personalities. And like many children of the seventies, I viewed life through a prism of popular culture, movies, and TV. I'd say to my friends things like "Doesn't that guy look like Dean Wormer from *Animal House*?" or "This gathering reminds me of the dinner scene in *Moonstruck*." Movies also helped me recall and define periods in my life. For instance, I'd never forget Christmas Day in 1977 at the Kent Theatre on Coney Island Avenue in Flatbush, since that was where and when I saw *Saturday Night Fever,* my first R-rated film.

When we were children, my parents forbade us kids to watch more than an hour of television per day. It made me hunger for television all the more. (Never place strict limitations on a child, as this breeds lifelong desire.) I'd wake up at six in the morning on Sundays and quietly sit in the dark, clad in my Batman pajamas, on the cold, tiled floor in the den inches from the big black-and-white Zenith so I could turn down the volume in case I heard my parents coming. It was bliss as I watched back-to-back half hours of *The Little Rascals, Davey and Goliath, Bugs Bunny,* and *Abbott and Costello.* I always envied friends who had their own television sets in their bedrooms.

I also knew more about television and movie trivia than about any school subject. I remember reading a news article about a prisoner in a Boston jail who scaled a five-story wall to the jail's roof and announced that he wouldn't come down until the corrections officers named for him all six children in the Brady Bunch family. None of the officers could oblige, though he eventually climbed down. My reaction was disbelief. Not at the convict's actions, but at the guards who couldn't name the Brady kids.

I first learned of career paths in Hollywood through several articles that spoke in idyllic fashion of the dream jobs available in the film industry. A piece in the *New York Times* called "Aspiring Moguls Take MBAs to Hollywood" particularly impressed me. I saved this yellowed, dog-eared clipping, reading and rereading about MBAs who had gotten creative jobs in the studios—testament to the power and influence of the press. I'm sure that each glowing article like that impelled another five thousand people in the United States to make a drastic career change.

So I leapt from my futon that night, adrenaline pumping, sure that I had arrived at my ultimate purpose in life. No single, pivotal event led me to this conclusion. But like a blurry image that gradually comes into focus, it seemed unassailable. It was an unformed, inchoate plan, to be sure, but it felt so right. First, business school in northern California, then a studio job in Los Angeles, with the goal of eventually becoming a producer. I had to share this epiphany with someone.

I turned on the lights and called Alexandra, one of my best friends at Merrill Lynch. We chased away the Sunday night doldrums each week by going to the movies. Afterward, we'd sit in a cafe and dissect the film like Siskel and Ebert, often getting into heated arguments.

"Hullo?"

"I'm going to change my life!"

"Who is it—Everett?" she said groggily. "What time is it?"

"It's a quarter to one...But listen, I finally know what I want to do in life...the movies. I'm going to try and break into the movie industry as a creative executive. I'm so pumped up—I had to call!"

"That's great! Listen, umm...call me in the morning and we'll talk." But she was merely humoring me. Disappointed, I realized that no one but I could understand the revelation I had had and the conviction that I was going to redirect the course of my life. One tends to be melodramatic at age twenty-three.

It was no surprise that I was being inexorably drawn toward Hollywood. Hollywood, like Wall Street in the mid-1980s, was where the opportunistic overachievers were heading like moths drawn to street lamps. But I was always a tad too late. The baby boomers had arrived beforehand and taken the best for themselves. I had chosen investment banking in the late eighties only to see the market crash and the gravy dry up. In a different decade, I probably would have gone on to law school after college. But who wouldn't have tried to enter a field that promised so much so quickly to a young graduate? (Never offer an easy fix to a child of the television generation—it's no contest.) A starting salary of $30,000 a year, plus bonus, travel, and a front-row seat to the most exciting business of the time. In 1986, Wall Street seemed to be at the epicenter of the business world.

"Where do I sign up?" was my thought, though as a political

science major I scarcely knew a thing about finance. "Don't worry about that," the investment bankers reassured me over dinners at four-star restaurants. "We'll teach you all you need to know in our training programs. As long as you're intelligent and well groomed, went to the right school, and got excellent grades, we want you." That's why fellow inductees in my year at Merrill Lynch included people with such majors as art history, biology, Far Eastern studies, and philosophy. When we met each other in the training program, we marveled at our diversity. ("How unusual, you say you actually studied *economics* in college?")

But we knew in our hearts that something was askew. Forget about junk bonds, real estate speculation, S&L defaults, insider trading scandals—we knew before anyone else of the incipient downfall for the eighties and for Wall Street. Our very recruitment meant trouble ahead for the industry! Most of us should have been in law school, medical school, or the arts, or volunteering or bumming around Europe, but, most importantly, pursuing our passions. Certainly, we should not have been working twelve to fourteen hours a day, including weekends, punching numbers into a computer. To be sure, we traveled first class, rode limousines home, and ate out on company expense accounts every night. But we were still relatively poor and only making slightly more than minimum wage when you factored in our work schedule.

I never did get to taste the spoils of the eighties. The October 19, 1987, stock market crash put an end to my illusions. Name your cliché, but it *was* too good to be true—there was no free lunch. But I was spoiled by the time the two-year analyst stint was over, and I grimaced at the prospect of starting anew as a grunt in Hollywood. Perhaps, I hoped, my graduate degree would allow me to skip a few rungs. So once again, I chose the easy route and went on to business school—just when it seemed like everyone and his mother was getting an MBA, to the tune of sixty-seven thousand newly minted MBAs in 1990.

At least I got into Stanford. Stanford seemed different from other business schools. It was the school of choice for those who questioned the very conventions of the mainstream business world while working within its confines. With strong links to Silicon Valley and alumni like Phil Knight, founder of Nike, and Scott McNealy, founder of Sun Microsystems, it had a well-earned reputation as a hotbed of entrepreneurship. And, not insignificantly, it was located in northern California. I think the photo in the recruiting brochure of the student typing on a laptop, wearing sunglasses and clad in shorts and T-shirt, with an Olympic-sized swimming pool in the background, was what clinched it for me. It took me several months, though, to get used to the fact that palm trees, golf, and windsurfing could coexist on a university campus. I kept waiting for "the catch."

And now, after business school, I was part of the throng seeking admission into the Hollywood carnival. The attraction was as much living in L.A. as working in the movie industry. The place and the industry reinforced each other's identity until they were nearly inseparable. Even though less than 5 percent of the city's residents worked directly in film, the industry pervaded the city both psychically and financially.

Besides, Los Angeles seemed to be the city of the nineties. The richest and most populous metropolitan area in the U.S., the busiest port, the largest retail market, the fastest-growing large city, and the gateway to the Pacific. It appeared to me that the center of gravity had shifted from the decaying east coast to the thriving west.

And, if you wanted entertainment, the mecca was L.A., with more than two-thirds of all feature films, dramatic series, and situation comedies produced there. Entertainment was also one of the few industries where people could reinvent themselves, regardless of their prior background or age. No one forgets that Irving Thalberg was twenty-four when he headed MGM's production department. Of course, a corollary to this was that many of Hollywood's top executives like Barry Diller, then chairman of Fox, Jeffrey Katzenberg, then chairman of Walt Disney's motion picture group, Ron Meyer, president of Creative Artists Agency, and producer Scott Rudin had skipped college altogether.

My first taste of Hollywood came in the summer between years at business school, when I landed one of the coveted summer positions and worked at Paramount Pictures as a financial analyst in the studio's home video division. The demand from business school students for these summer jobs was such that the studios could offer $500 a week and still get hundreds of resumés. I eagerly accepted the job, though my classmates working at consulting firms or investment banks were making over $1,000 a week plus a summer-end bonus.

That summer, I walked through the studio gates each day, but I might as well have been a janitor as far as the creative community was concerned. I was one of the numbers people, the "suits," and thoroughly tangential to the moviemaking process. A major part of my job involved calculating how many videocassettes of a given film we needed to sell in order to break even on the manufacturing costs and the advances given to the film's producers. The ironic part was that we used to calculate returns on investment *after* the fact; that is, the studio's creative executives and lawyers would travel to the film festivals, negotiate with the producers, and then, as an afterthought, hand the signed contracts to the financial types, as if to say, "Oh, by the way, will we be making a profit on this deal?"

Each day I typed spreadsheets into the computer, the same work I had done on Wall Street. Only this time, instead of IBM or General Electric at the top of the spreadsheet, it was *Raiders of the Lost Ark* or *Top Gun*. I stared at computer screens like this one for nine hours a day:

	A	B		C
1		**NINJA WARRIORS 8**		
2				
3	TOTAL UNITS SOLD	100,000	110,000	120,000
4	Unit Retail Price	$79.95	$79.95	$79.95
5	Less: Discount	37.00%	37.00%	37.00%
6	Wholesale Price	$50.37	$50.37	$50.37
7	WHOLESALE REVENUES	$5,037,000	$5,540,700	$6,044,400
8	DISTRIBUTION FEE	1,511,100	1,662,210	1,813,320
9	LESS COSTS:			
10	Duplication	400,000	440,000	480,000
11	Packaging	25,000	27,500	30,000
12	Freight	19,000	20,900	22,800
13	Marketing	756,000	831,600	907,200
14				
15	TOTAL COSTS	1,200,000	1,320,000	1,440,000
16	LESS: RETURNS @ 15%	755,550	831,105	906,660
17	RETURNS PROCESSING FEE	3,000	3,300	3,600

The frustration was magnified: working in an atmosphere of creativity and excitement but only allowed to do the least enjoyable tasks. I learned from the Paramount experience that there was no reason for me to be in Hollywood if I wasn't working on the creative side where the film projects were developed. Of course there was still the pleasure of being able to tell friends with mundane jobs that I worked at a movie studio, which sounded ultra-glamorous to them. They imagined lunching at Spago, hobnobbing with celebrities, and in spare moments assisting producers with casting decisions. My friends, fascinated with Hollywood, wanted to believe the fantasy. I, on the other hand, felt a bit dishonest when they fawned over me. It was like being a floor sweeper in the Lamborghini factory. I was getting admired for the part of the business I was miles away from.

I also learned that the chance of switching over from the financial side to the creative was infinitesimal. The overwhelming consensus of studio executives I spoke with was that I'd have a better chance of getting discovered by a talent scout in a pharmacy.

When I say the creative area, I don't mean directing or acting. I had my heart set on becoming a producer. This seemed to be the position at the nexus of the business and creative worlds. My financial background would be invaluable, as each movie project represented a new business start-up for the producer. And the idea of risking tens of millions of dollars and several years on a project whose success would be determined in one weekend was extremely alluring to me.

But since I lacked the necessary contacts in the creative community as well as the access to capital, I could not immediately hang my name on a shingle and call myself a producer (though many in Hollywood did just this). My immediate goal, therefore, was to land a position as a creative executive, a nebulous title for those studio executives who shepherded film projects from script through production, representing the studio's interests vis-à-vis producers, actors, and agents. At senior levels, creative executives scouted for new material and competed for hot scripts, then, once a script was bought, they "developed" it—which meant selecting those elements, like actors and a director, needed to maximize box office revenues.

That summer at Paramount, I met with Teddy Zee, a thirty-year-old Harvard MBA who was a production VP at the studio. Zee's office at Paramount made me crave his job: no computers or calculators, just stacks of scripts, a color TV and VCR, framed movie posters, and film memorabilia. Zee and the other creative executives also wore the coolest outfits—all the hip Hugo Boss suits and bold ties I saw pictured in *GQ* magazine but had never dared wear in a business setting.

As Zee told me, development was the one area on the creative side that hired MBAs. Zee, who had initially worked at Touche Ross Consulting out of business school, assured me that my business background would not be held against me. These positions, after all, demanded management skills. And when production executives inevitably became producers, they surely needed to understand the financing aspects of filmmaking.

"Hey, aren't we learning here in business school how to be *creative* executives?" I asked my classmates. And boy, did they love the idea. They showered me with their approbation. Their career choices—management consulting, investment banking, brand management—all paled in comparison to creative executive at a movie studio in Los Angeles. Working in the movies amidst palm trees and sunshine was just as much their fantasy as it was mine.

"That is *so* cool," they said. "Just remember us when you're a bigshot movie producer and you're on that stage accepting the Oscar for best picture." I joked along with them, for I firmly believed that this success was just a matter of time. It was my destiny.

And with destiny propelling me, I made all the necessary plans to move my life and outlook from New York to Los Angeles.

CHAPTER 3

The Journey

*One doesn't discover new lands without consenting
to lose sight of the shore for a very long time.*

ANDRÉ GIDE

I was in a hurry to begin my new life in L.A. The day after graduation, I flew back to New York for one week to pack up my belongings and see my parents. It was also important for me to see New York again and reaffirm my desire to leave. Accentuating the negatives of the city, I figured, would propel me to embrace L.A. all the more.

On my first day back, I traveled into Manhattan from my parents' house in Brooklyn to get a haircut. Aboard the R train to Greenwich Village, I gripped the metal handle and swayed as we hurtled underground through Brooklyn neighborhoods. The movement of the train was hypnotic, and I was soon lost in thoughts of my move west. Suddenly, the train jolted to a stop, pitching me against a large man at least a foot taller, who glared down at me. I grabbed hold of his arm to steady myself, muttered an apology, and quickly looked away, hoping this wasn't the action that would cause him to snap. As sweat trickled down the side of my head, I scanned the array of advertisements for roach spray, laser surgery, and secretarial school.

We pulled into the crowded Cortlandt Street station, and the doors sprang open. I was instantly ejected from the car by the surging crowd. Standing near the door, I tried to gauge the best moment to dash back on board. As the exodus slowed, I was pushed inside and spun into an awkward position, wedged between two people. Gradually, I realized that the old and withered woman in front of me was slowly but surely grinding her behind against my crotch. She looked over her shoulder and smiled, flashing a gap-toothed grin.

Thankfully, we soon pulled into my stop, and I forcefully pried myself free. "Rrraaathh Breethh," the conductor announced on the sound system, or "Eighth Street" in unamplified sound. Weaving skillfully through the crowd, I was one of the first to exit the station. As I passed through the turnstile, a glaring troll-like man carrying a placard shouted, "Repent—Jesus says a big earthquake is coming!" I smiled at this "only in New York" scene and quickened my pace, sidestepping an old black man in a wheelchair who sat at the entrance and yelled at passersby when they denied him their spare change.

I entered Astor Place Haircutters and made my way through the labyrinth of immigrant barbers and mirrored stalls, clearing a path through hair of all colors and textures, which blanketed the black and white linoleum tile floor. Astor Place is a barber shop in Greenwich Village famed for punk haircuts, low prices, and a no-frills atmosphere. Novices who arrive at the door without a barber in mind are slightly rattled when the manager shouts out: "Who's free?" My barber, Valentino, whom I had been going to since high school, was a short, cheerful Romanian who was much more talented than his slovenly surroundings indicated.

"Everick!" cried Valentino, his face lighting up. "Good to see you. Why you no come by 'til now?" I hadn't been to see him since winter break, but he always made his customers feel as if he had been counting the days until their next haircut. In a hurry, I ignored the niceties and smiled. "Hey, Valentino! How many people before me?" I wasn't certain, but I think I unconsciously adopted a slight Romanian accent while in his presence.

He smiled a semi-insane smile and held up his left thumb and index finger. "Only two," he replied, crossing out a name and adding mine to the list on the crumpled napkin on his mantel.

His current patient, a young black woman, frowned at him. He noticed and quickly resumed his work. She stared defiantly at the mirror as he resumed shearing her head like a shrub. He ran the razor back and forth along her hair, slowly forming a perfect square. Valentino kept looking anxiously from her hair to her angry expression reflected in the mirror. Still, the man was the Botticelli of barbers, and when he finished she rewarded him with a surprisingly beautiful smile.

A college-age brunette with "big hair" and raspberry-colored lips immediately leaped into the seat, chewing gum furiously and pulling at her hair while staring intently at the mirror.

"Christ, I bin waitin' for half an hour, Valenteeeno!"

"Don't worry, Vicky," he soothed as he simultaneously draped a smock over her and tried to kiss her on the cheek. "I give you special treatment." With that he winked at me and furiously began cutting.

When it was my turn, I hopped into the seat as Valentino whirled the smock around me.

"You want same thing, right?" He wrapped tissue paper around my neck (I never questioned why).

"Yeah, but not too short." We said the same lines every time.

He sprayed my hair with water and combed it back. "Hey, what you goin' do after feenish business school?" He had a better memory for my career than most of my relatives, though he saw me but six or seven times a year. Actually, that was a lot more often than I saw my relatives. They still asked questions like what grade I was in. "I'm done with school—I just graduated last week." He beamed at me. "Oh, con-glatulations, Everick!" "Thanks." I smiled, but felt old sitting in the same chair in which he had congratulated me on both my high school and college graduations. "I'm thinking of going to Hollywood and working in the movies." I was curious to hear the commonsensical wisdom he would inevitably impart. He had a keen mind and often made astute observations about current political and social issues.

He continued cutting, and I thought he hadn't heard me. He abruptly paused. "Ah, John Wayne, Jack Nicholson, Steve McQueen. And Everick! You send me picture for mirror." He pointed at the mélange of publicity photos of actors which lined the borders of his mirror, none of whom I recognized. Valentino's Hall of Fame: a sure guarantee of career anonymity.

I shook my head and smiled. "No, no—I don't want to act. I want to be a producer...You know, read scripts and decide which films to make."

"Ohhh." He stopped cutting to reflect on this, his eyes alive with concentration. He looked at me in the mirror, oblivious to the crowd waiting impatiently behind us. "Is very tough business. Crazy peoples. Snob." He tapped his finger under his nose to emphasize the point. He gripped my shoulder as he continued. "But, are very rich, have beautiful women, sunshine all year. Is very good for peoples with power."

I laughed. "You got that right."

I was on autopilot that whole week at home, preparing for the move. Sweating in the June heat in my bedroom on the third floor, I packed up boxes and sent them via UPS to my friend Mitch's house in

Woodland Hills, a town in the San Fernando Valley near Los Angeles. Mitch was one of my roommates in a house four of us shared in Palo Alto during our second year at business school. An L.A. native, he was testament to the evolving image of business school students. His typical attire at school consisted of black sunglasses, a cut-off black jersey touting assorted British punk rock groups, gym shorts, and black hi-top Converse sneakers. I identified with Mitch since he too was pursuing an alternative career path, having landed a coveted position in music publishing at Bertelsmann Music Group. Though the job was based in New York, I was happy to learn that he'd first spend six months in training in L.A. The plan was for me to fly to Los Angeles, find an apartment, and begin my job search, all before my belongings arrived at Mitch's in five days. He would then redirect the boxes to my new residence.

I was exhausted from all the last-minute errands by the time I boarded the American Airlines plane at JFK Airport on Sunday for the last flight of the night. As I passed the smiling stewardess at the plane's entrance hatch, I turned to my left and looked wistfully at the plush, spacious first-class section, where there was a festive, clubby atmosphere. Three banker types were huddled to one side laughing and drinking champagne, trying their hardest to look relaxed. I knew the whole routine: "What can I get for you, sir? Champagne, orange juice, or mimosa?"

The perks of investment banking had spoiled me. I would not be eating caviar and getting hot washcloths for a while. Those days were over for now. That was fine with me. What mattered most was recovering the freedom I had given up for those perks. Let the bankers have the warm roasted cashews and the beluga, along with the eighty-hour work weeks. I'd eventually return to first class, but on my own terms. Until then, I'd be in the back of the plane with the other wannabes.

Continuing down the aisle, I perked up as I noticed that I'd be sitting across from three blond sorority types who were happily applying lipstick and eye shadow in unison.

I pulled out my current reading: *The Movie Business Book*. I slowly looked to my side when I noticed my neighbor across the aisle reading the title.

"Oh, are you in the business?" she gushed. I paused to think. Was I? "Yeah, I guess you could say I'm a producer in training." That sounded all right.

Five hours later, the four of us knew all the salient points of each other's lives. Pam, Stacy, and Joanne were juniors at USC and had spent the first few weeks of their summer break in Manhattan. I was excited when they gave me their phone numbers and told me they threw lots of parties. I was already building myself a social base in L.A.

We were all talked out, however, as the plane began its descent. I stared out the plastic porthole, mesmerized by the twinkling white, yellow, and red lights of the city, spread out below us like a massive LED display.

Exiting the baggage claim area, I dropped my bags on the crosswalk, enjoying the balmy evening air. With the many joyous reunions taking place around me, I half expected someone to shout out my name (in a slow-motion scene of me running into the arms of a blonde, perhaps played by Claudia Schiffer).

I jarred myself back to reality and crossed the street to catch the airport shuttle van; there was too much at stake to dawdle now.

"Destinations!" called out the clean-cut surfer type, with a red bandanna wrapped around his head tourniquet-style, who was driving the bright blue SuperShuttle van.

"Sheraton." "Best Western." "Shangri-La." I quickly called out, "Santa Monica Youth Hostel," while looking out the window as we headed north on the 405 freeway. One day, I reassured myself, I would instead be chauffeured to my beachfront mansion in Malibu.

After checking in at the hostel, I stowed my bags in the spartan but clean room, flopped down on the bunk bed, and tried to sleep. Thoughts of my farewell to my parents, however, were racing through my mind. I knew that my visit home to Brooklyn would weaken my sense of determination and fortitude.

The words of my father reverberated in my ear. That's the beauty of parents—you don't even need them to be present in order to hear their lectures. Instant guilt and rebuke whenever you need it.

"You must be out of your freakin' mind!" my father screamed from the top of the stairs. "For what reason are you running away, *three thousand miles* away? For what reason?" He was great at repeating phrases for emphasis. "To be a producer? You must be crazy. What normal person with no experience tries to become a producer? What got into you?"

I should explain that my father's frame of reference was our orthodox Jewish neighborhood in Brooklyn, as homogeneous and provincial as any small town in middle America. Jewish children in Flatbush had a choice of five professions: doctor/dentist, lawyer, accountant, teacher, or banker/stockbroker. Anything outside of those careers was deemed deviant. Fashion—for homosexuals. Journalism—what does it pay? Advertising—that's for the *goyim*. And the movie industry—you'd have to be a *meshuganah* to even try to enter such a flaky business.

"I'm just testing the waters," I replied absentmindedly, while checking my bags downstairs in the foyer.

"You can test the waters from here. Where all your friends and family are."

My heart was starting to ache as I waited in the kitchen with my mother for the taxi to arrive. I had listened to countless variations of this refrain over the last six months, though he was clearly at an apex of emotion tonight.

"Don't worry, you'll be fine," my mother said, with a look of sadness in her eyes. "You're going to have that town eating out of your hand. You're the best, the best. You know that, don't you?"

I smiled at her, unsure how she could be so confident. My father's tirade continued upstairs. "An Ivy League education, a cushy Wall Street job, a Stanford MBA—what the hell got into you? You must be out of your mind. The trouble with you is you didn't know how good you had it. You were spoiled on first-class this and first-class that. Some people would kill for that." He slammed his bedroom door hard. I knew that he'd reopen it in under thirty seconds.

"Shhhhhhh," my mother soothed while embracing me and rubbing my back. "Don't listen to him, I believe in you." I hugged her, noticing that her body seemed to be getting smaller with age.

The door upstairs flew open with a bang. "A fifty-thousand-dollar MBA—for what, for what? For suckers like my son, that's who—that's who!"

Just then, I heard his heavy footsteps coming down the stairs. Though he was slower at age sixty, those were the same pounding steps that used to strike terror in my heart when I was a child. I knew that anger and punishment were not far behind. As the third of four, I suffered from middle-child syndrome and was constantly testing the limit of my father's authority.

He appeared in the kitchen doorway and I braced myself now for the attack. His eyes were wild, his face and balding head flushed; he was in a full state of fury. He was short, but his excess weight made him seem huge to me when I was a child. Now he looked almost comical, standing bare-footed in his undershirt and polka-dotted, size 44 boxer shorts.

He pointed at me. "I'm warning you, I'm warning you," he said, invoking his harshest weapon. "If you step out of this house, I won't support you and your idiotic plans."

"I don't need your goddam money! I have plenty of savings." *That* was an exaggeration of my current account balance, mostly depleted after a very expensive MBA.

I turned to my mother. "God, you'd think I was going to Russia or something."

"For God's sake, Lenny, leave him alone already!" she yelled. "You can't live his life for him."

That was all he was waiting for. He turned his wrath on her. "This is *your* fault! *Your* fault! You encourage him and his wacko ideas! You always have."

Yin and yang. That's the way it has always been with my parents. They invariably took opposite positions on any topic, from politics to choice of breakfast cereal. This led to some spectacular fights on the most trivial of trivialities: "Sylvia, why are there two brands of cream cheese in the refrigerator?" Growing up with them was like riding a seesaw, the two counteracting influences and forces shaping my personality. I knew that I had pursued investment banking when I finished college partly to please my father. Throughout my analyst stint, he had reveled in my tales of Wall Street wealth and power. I also knew that in choosing the movie industry, I was now moving more toward my mother's point of view.

My mother, ever the creative free spirit, pushed me to pursue dreams and try anything new just for the experience. She was an English teacher who worked with high school students on developing their creativity and writing talents. My father was a criminal-defense lawyer who saw human failings every day up close. A nose-to-the-grindstone cynic, he advised me to play it safe or face certain failure. Of course, if I followed his advice to the letter, I'd have spent most of my spare moments at home, as he did, in front of the television watching *Jeopardy!*

He resumed his tirade, for a new line of attack was forming in his mind: the "history" theory. As a criminal attorney, he was excellent at building a case against someone. "You have a history of doing schmucky things, you know. A history." That's my dad—he never failed to invoke mistakes made over the last fifteen years.

"You have a history," he repeated. "This is no different from the firecrackers, the drugs, the suspension." These were a litany of my worst offenses, all committed before age sixteen, invoked whenever I did anything he disagreed with. "This is just one more of your jerky ideas."

"I'm sorry you feel that way," I replied. "But whether you like it or not, I'm leaving. So you better get used to it and wish me good luck." I suddenly glimpsed the headlights of the taxi through the dining room windows. My mother noticed at the same time and loudly announced, "Taxi's here!"

I quickly grabbed my bags, kissed her on the cheek, and opened the front door as my father continued shouting behind me. "You're making a huge mistake. A huge mistake. The biggest mistake of your life!"

I could hear them fighting as I sadly walked to the taxi. I hated to leave at such a lousy moment, but was unwilling to stay and be yelled at for one second longer.

Still, as I lay in bed at the youth hostel I couldn't help but wonder if I had made a serious error. This was my *life* I was playing with. I soon drifted to sleep and had one of my famous anxiety dreams, which involved me ripping my contact lenses over and over again.

I awoke with a start, feeling disoriented and sweaty in the heat of the day. I heard voices, and as my eyes focused I recalled where I was. Three cheerful, ruddy German backpackers were expeditiously packing and heading out for the day. I longed to be part of their group, with only the mild thoughts of that day's sightseeing plans.

CHAPTER 4

A New Life

Look with favor upon a new beginning.

VIRGIL

My apartment building on Wilshire Boulevard was like one of those seedy motels in Miami Beach where my family used to stay when we visited our grandparents. All it was missing was a neon VACANCY sign out front and an ice machine. I liked it, nonetheless, because it was one of the few remaining three-story ranch-style buildings amidst the many sterile high-rises along Wilshire. The jewel of this building was the inner courtyard with a small swimming pool surrounded by leafy palms.

It had taken me just two days to sublet this furnished one-bedroom apartment, which I found through an announcement on a bulletin board at UCLA. The apartment was in Westwood, the heart of L.A.'s west side and the upper-middle-class neighborhood surrounding UCLA where ex–New Yorkers seemed to feel at home. After all, Westwood Village, the collection of stores and movie theaters near the college, was L.A.'s only pedestrian community.

The apartments in my building were occupied by two types of

tenants. The first were suspicious old ladies, the kind who shoplifted T-bone steaks at the supermarket and locked their doors as you passed their apartment. They never said hello, preferring to scowl when they walked by. The others were young professionals with some connection to the entertainment industry, none of whom had positions good enough to afford to move elsewhere.

On Saturdays and Sundays, seven or eight regulars lounged around the pool until about three in the afternoon, when the shadows of the flanking high-rises passed over the courtyard like an eclipse. They sunbathed and exchanged gossip from the week past. My living room window faced the courtyard, and I'd periodically peer between the slats of the venetian blinds like a latter-day Jimmy Stewart in *Rear Window,* and wait until an attractive woman lay outside. What a strange feeling to leave your apartment dressed in bathing suit and thongs, carrying a towel and suntan lotion, and file past mailboxes to the courtyard. Often, I'd have to squeeze past the old woman next door in 3G who spent hours slowly walking back and forth on the faded brown carpet in the dim and musty hallway hunched over a metal walker. I had long given up on getting any response from her. The sight always chilled me, and I usually went the long way around the circular hallway.

There was camaraderie among the denizens at the pool. We were all transplanted from the East Coast and now found ourselves in this strange city where every day was a beach day. We were also wannabes, and we commiserated with each other on our efforts to break into the industry. But mostly we'd lie there in the sun, listen to Top Forty radio on KIIS FM and discuss the most inane topics, like old TV sitcoms (typical would be a heated debate over who was prettier, Marsha Brady or Laurie Partridge), exercise regimens, and pets. Dogs were a frequent subject; one of the tenants had a bull terrier named Oscar that became the mascot of the pool, and we fawned over him shamelessly.

So I was living in a not-so-cool apartment house in a not-so-happening part of the city. That was strike one in L.A. Strike two was my car: I drove a metallic gray 1981 Toyota Corolla hatchback, possibly one of the least hip cars on earth. And finally, strike three was my near-empty Rolodex, in a city in which connections were your most important assets. I did have several friends, classmates from business school, cousins of cousins, friends of friends—but no one in the industry I could count on or who would call me first.

I was nonetheless quite optimistic. The sheer boldness of my action impressed and excited me; it was the first time in my life that I had taken such risk. This was all about destiny and beating the odds, about finally taking the reins of my life and saying, "Enough of taking the safe route!" My father would soon be proven wrong. I was going to make it here based on my intelligence, street smarts, and, above all, perseverance. I would carve out a new identity for myself in L.A., and none of the naysayers could stop me.

The first step in a movie industry job search is to identify every contact you might have in the entertainment business, no matter how tangential. I listed every alumnus from my college and business school, every relative or friend of a friend. I was a fiend for collecting names, even from articles and books. I also obtained lists of USC and UCLA business school alumni, figuring at least we had the MBA in common.

And then I called all of them, mostly leaving messages with their assistants. I soon learned that copious record keeping was essential, given the volume of calls I was making. I would be on line with one executive, and my call waiting would beep.

"Hi, this is Susan Farkas, returning your call." I had no idea who this person was.

"Oh, hiiiii. Can you hold on for a sec?" I would then frantically rummage through my notes with papers flying in the air, trying to find out who she was and how I knew her.

I learned to jot down notes of every conversation or contact that I had with an executive, including the assistant's name and, most importantly, the name of the person who referred me to my target.

For the first two months, every day of my job search was similar. I treated it like a full-time job, writing letters and making calls during the work day. Having a daily routine helped me feel productive. I loved talking to myself as if I were my own secretary as I sat in front of a desk dressed in undershorts and T-shirt. "Everett, can you get me a Diet Coke," or "Ev, hon, can you get so-and-so on the phone?"

Aside from personal contacts, the outsider's other invaluable resource is the *Hollywood Creative Directory:* the guide to every production company in town, with the names and titles of every development and production executive in film and television, including produced credits. I bought a copy and quickly realized why they update the directory every four months: It becomes obsolete the day after it's published. The movement of people between production companies is chaotic, and the tracking of it an art. Daily supplements would be more useful. That's why the trade papers come in handy.

Don't get me started on the trades. It's a truly strange industry whose two major trade publications read like *People* magazine. I got a kick out of hearing people argue the pros and cons of *Daily Variety* and the *Hollywood Reporter*. It was so patently obvious to me that they both featured the same articles published in different formats, as if a brilliant but cynical publisher owned both magazines and figured out that formatting and language style were vastly more important than content. (The analytical side of me had to find out: Actually, *Variety* is owned by a British company, Reed Publishing, while the *Hollywood Reporter* is owned by a Dutch concern, VNU.) I think Hollywood executives were thrilled by being able to read both of their morning papers in ten minutes and feel remarkably accomplished by nine A.M. Each studio executive merited his or her own copy, even though colleagues sitting several feet away would be done with theirs in five minutes.

At seventy-five cents per copy per day, however, the trades were strictly luxuries for me. That's why I drove every day to the nearby 7-Eleven on Santa Monica Boulevard and quietly stood and read the trades near the Slurpee machine, hoping the Indian counterman wouldn't say anything. Though he never bothered me, I kept hallucinating and seeing Apu from *The Simpsons:* "Hey you, meester, this is not a reading library, you know." I even used the store's coin-operated photocopy machine to copy the classified ads.

My route back to my apartment from the store took me past the smoking-deaths billboard on Santa Monica Boulevard, which featured a digital display: "383,185 smoking deaths this year and counting." I began to morosely chart the passage of time by the number of smoking deaths that had elapsed. I calculated that each day of my job search was worth approximately 1,190 deaths. It helped put things in perspective.

Back at the apartment, I then marked down in the *Creative Directory* which industry people had moved where. I hummed to myself, enjoying this busywork, and before long my copy was filled with scribbles and crossed-out lines. Still, it was my bible, and I loved it in a weird way.

And there was nothing like the *Directory* for bullshitting. It instantly made me seem like I knew of everyone in Hollywood.

"You should talk to Castle Rock," someone would advise me.

"Who?" I would reply, while flipping in fast-forward to the Castle Rock page. "Bob Cohen or Sam Schwartz?"

"Definitely Schwartz, especially since Cohen left last week for Tri-Star."

"No, that's incredible—do you mean that Bob . . . " (I'd stall before finding Tri-Star) " . . . replaced Kelly Matthews?"

"Nah, Kelly was promoted to VP."

And so on. See what I mean, though? You would have thought on the other end of the phone that I actually knew the entire town. Most probably, both of us were frauds, flipping in tandem through the book.

No matter how good a schmoozer you were, however, nothing

could be arranged without befriending the executives' assistants. My trick was to use the person's first name as often as possible while we were talking and to mention details from prior conversations, which I had recorded in my notes. It instilled a false sense of camaraderie between us. "Hi, Tina, it's Everett Weinberger again...By the way, Tina, did you ever give away your dog's puppies?... That's so funny! Listen, Tina, I just wanted to check if Bill had a chance to read my letter yet."

I chatted this way with an assistant at music industry mogul David Geffen's film production company, and to my surprise she quickly scheduled a meeting for me with her boss, Cari-Esta Albert, the top production executive there. I arrived at their well-appointed offices on Sunset Boulevard and immediately began schmoozing with the assistant like we were old friends. After all, I thought, I had charmed her into getting me the meeting. I *must* be hot stuff.

While I was waiting, another guy walked in and loudly announced himself. "Hi, I'm Eric Weinberg. I have a ten o'clock with Cari-Esta." Oh, oh. I felt myself shrinking in size, for I knew his name sounded a tad too close to mine. Sure enough, the assistant, my pal, had inadvertently mixed my name up with his when she had told me to come right in. The true appointment was not with Everett Weinberger, the starving hopeful, but with Eric Weinberg, the successful writer. As a footnote, though, the assistant felt she owed me one, and eventually secured me a meeting.

Another trick I had of reaching executives on the phone was to call during off-peak hours when their assistants were not in. Often this meant calling before eight in the morning or after seven at night. Though they were usually annoyed that I had pierced their security buffer, at least I had them on the phone for the pitch.

Phone calls were most effective when I had some connection, no matter how tenuous or far-fetched, to the executive. The top executives at the studios, however, were way out of my reach. Figuring I was somewhat creative and a decent writer, I reasoned that a letter-writing campaign would get their attention.

Using my trusty *Creative Directory*, I targeted virtually all the power brokers in Hollywood's studios and production companies. I concocted what I thought was an intriguing opening line: "Out of the 328 Stanford MBAs who graduated in June, only one is pursuing motion picture development. I am that one." Of course, my father would have said, "Sure you're that one—you're the only putz who would throw away an MBA to become a producer!"

Most executives in Hollywood who took my call agreed to meet with me after I indicated that I was calling for advice and not for a job. I must have met over one hundred people in three months. Many even treated me to breakfast or lunch, courtesy of movie studio expense accounts.

Before each meeting or interview, I conducted extensive research on the executive I was meeting. Since every production executive gets at least nominal mention in *Variety* and *Hollywood Reporter* with each job change (probably every year and a half on average), it was not hard to quickly investigate their backgrounds. My best resource was the clippings file in the library of the Academy of Motion Picture Arts and Sciences in Beverly Hills. The details proved invaluable, if only to impress them with my thoroughness. I once stunned Jane Sindell, a top agent at Creative Artists Agency, when I nonchalantly asked her about a boating accident she had gotten into seven years before, and disclosed that I knew her license plate used to spell SHMOOZE.

During those first few months of my search, I was always on the go and loved this frenetic pace. Back-to-back breakfast, lunch, and afternoon meetings. I'd race from studio to studio, Beverly Hills to Burbank, Universal City to Hollywood. Hell, I felt like a player. Surely *something* had to come from all those meetings.

But one meeting per contact was all I got. Follow-up calls were usually left unreturned. Why did the executives bother meeting with me? It was probably a mixture of duty to newcomers, paying off favors to friends, and, in no small way, ego. And Hollywood executives must get a lot of satisfaction when they realize how many people want their job. No matter how miserable or insignificant their position, they have to feel smug when resumés and phone calls are directed at them from strangers, all begging to meet with them. For the most part, the creative executives' advice was laughable, mainly because there was very little advice one could give the uninitiated. There was an infinite number of ways to get a job on the creative side in Hollywood, every one of them a long shot. Each movie executive, it seemed, had taken a unique route, and serendipity always played an important role.

"Read the trades," many would tell me, as if they were giving me the tablets from Sinai. Or, "Become an agent." But what I was really there for, unspoken as it might have been, was to beg for a personal reference or job leads. I was a complete stranger to them, and yet I needed them to like me enough to toss me a bone. Maybe a few contacts to call or the name and number of someone they'd heard was looking to hire. Anything. It felt pathetic to be in such a weak position while my friends from school were negotiating $25,000 signing bonuses or taking round-the-world summer trips.

Some executives were philosophical. "My yoga teacher once told me that life is like being inside a crystal cube," began one senior vice president of production at Paramount. "You are in the middle of this glass-walled cube and emit beams of light, which bounce against the crystal walls. So you have to stay centered in the cube, and the light beams will then eventually bounce back to you. In other words, if you emit good, positive energy, eventually it will be returned to you. And vice versa for bad energy." I sat in the chair and pensively nodded at him, like one of those bobbing-head dolls, wondering what he was trying to say. He then proceeded to tell me the studio was not interviewing for junior creative executives at the time, but I should hang in there.

Another production executive was equally creative. "It's like the Japanese board game of Go—you know, the board game with the black and white tiles. When you begin losing one sector of the board, it's best sometimes to abandon it and begin working on a totally different region. In this way, you can win that new area and then come back to reconquer the old sector." I suppose I looked dumbfounded, because the guy began explaining the connection.

I made a pilgrimage to nearly every MBA working on the creative side in Hollywood, hoping to exploit the implicit kinship I assumed that degree gave us. Most of them, however, spent part of the meeting explaining to me why they were different from "other" MBAs (*much* more creative), and why I should not get my hopes up. They also described their lucky break and made it sound like it was a million-to-one miracle. Most made sure to tell me how utterly irrelevant their degree was in Hollywood. It was the ultimate in hypocrisy when they decried the influx of MBAs in the industry.

Mark Adams, a thirty-two-year-old MBA and production executive at Disney, was typical of the lot. He was wearing a Hermès tie, probably from his days as an investment banker, with a preppy navy blazer, jeans, multi-patterned socks, and black Italian loafers—a fossil record of fashion styles from the past few years. He spoke of the terrific cut in pay he had suffered to come to Disney. He seemed painfully aware that his classmates in other professions were probably making a lot more than he was. Above all, he did not look very happy to me. Hollow was more like it. I mentioned that I had been doing some writing on the side and would love ultimately to write some scripts. As if on autopilot, he droned, "I like writers. I have a lot of respect for them. We definitely need more and better writers. Because good material is always the bait that catches the fish." And when I asked him if he ever used his MBA on the job, he pointed to the page number on an opened script on his desk and quipped, as if reading from a cue card, "The only numbers I see each day are these."

Occasionally, I'd attend meetings of the Stanford in Entertainment Club, a motley collection of young Stanford alumni in the industry who gathered with the undying hope that one of the prominent alums would show up. After all, the club president assured me, Gale Anne Hurd (producer of *The Terminator, Aliens,* and *The Abyss*), actress Sigourney Weaver, Ed Pressman (producer of *Wall*

Street), and Tom Pollock (chairman of Universal) were Stanford alumni and on the mailing list. You never know if they'll show, she told me.

These were impersonal gatherings, as none of the struggling wannabes wanted to waste time talking to another, while the moderately successful ones didn't want to be seen, and thus tainted by, talking to a wannabe. It was the sort of sniffing that dogs do when they pass another dog on the street. I'd inevitably end up getting cornered by some geek from Ventura who worked as a sound technician at a studio but was writing screenplays on the side. Whenever I did engage someone with a decent job in conversation, he or she soon developed a panicky look and began darting glances around the room, hoping to make a quick exit. It was an unwritten rule in Hollywood: You only spoke to someone at your level or higher (a Catch-22 for those at the bottom).

My mother provided me with the most oddball connections to industry people. She would say, "Your cousin Francis was childhood friends with his brother. He may not remember Francis, but mention that she went to Maimonides Hebrew School with his brother, Murray. They were in the same Talmud class." I actually called and met with the producer Howard Rosenman (*The Main Event, Lost Angels, Gross Anatomy*) because my mother reminded me that I had gone to Jewish sleep-away camp with his brother Sheppie (yes, Sheppie). And, on her advice, I ate at the Milky Way, a kosher dairy restaurant on Pico Boulevard in Beverly Hills owned by Steven Spielberg's mother, Leah Adler. The blintzes were good, but I was unsuccessful in exploiting the orthodox Jewish connection.

But the most peculiar meeting I had was with Rabbi Marvin Hier, head of the Simon Wiesenthal Center, an organization dedicated to promoting awareness of the Holocaust and to bringing Nazi war criminals to justice. A friend of a friend urged me to meet with him, hyping me on the fact that he had won an Oscar for the Holocaust documentary film *Genocide* and knew "tons of people" in the film industry.

The ironic part was that it took months to set up—it was actually harder to meet Rabbi Hier than the producers I called. Finally, after jousting with his harried assistant, I got an appointment. I walked into the Wiesenthal Center on Pico Boulevard, debating whether to wear a yarmulke or not. I put one on, figuring it was the equivalent of a power tie in other circles.

The rabbi was a short, fifty-one-year-old man whose lack of beard and aviator-style, gold-framed glasses made him look more like an accountant than a firebrand, activist rabbi. He asked me about my upbringing in Brooklyn and my yeshiva education. At that point, I would have shown him my circumcised penis if it would have helped get me a job. We discussed Israeli politics, and I made sure to express my support for the hawkish Likud party, knowing he would approve. I sprinkled my conversation with the requisite Hebrew and Yiddish words to impress upon him the "member of the tribe" connection. After ten minutes, he stood up to indicate that my time was up. He said that he would call this guy and that guy for me, and maybe also that guy and another guy, each a well-known film executive. I bobbed my head up and down enthusiastically and left convinced that I had befriended a genuine power player. In follow-up, however, he did nothing for me and never again took my calls.

One lesson I quickly learned was never to assume that an alumnus of my alma mater would care about me and my job search. I had courted Peter McAlevey, a Columbia College alum and produc-tion vice president at Stonebridge Entertainment, Michael Douglas's production company, for several months with letters and phone calls. He finally capitulated and agreed to meet with me, probably just to get me off his call list.

After I waited half an hour for him while sipping a Perrier (it was the law in Hollywood that guests had to be served mineral water), his office door burst open. Frenetic activity surrounded him as assistants and secretaries yelled messages at him and shoved documents in front of him to sign. As the tall, slim executive put on his beige, double-breasted Italian sport coat, he looked at me sitting quietly on the couch, like a teenager waiting for his date. "I've got an unscheduled meeting out of the office. Walk me to the parking lot." I was speechless as we walked out into the baking sun. He had poleaxed me with this display of rudeness.

As we walked on the hot asphalt driveway to his car, I broke the silence. "So, how'd you like Columbia?" I asked, squinting in the sun, hoping to evoke some warm college memories.

He looked down at me impassively through his sunglasses, not breaking stride. "You don't ask that kind of question when someone's about to get into their car," he said, stopping to open the door of his black, polished Jaguar.

"What kind of question *do* you ask?" I was irked and longed to tell him to fuck himself.

"You say to them, 'Nice car—can I have a job?'" And with that, he climbed in and was using his car phone before he had turned the car around. I was left standing in the parking lot by his empty space with the sun beaming down on me, shaking my head in disbelief. My imagination's film editor cut to an overhead shot to reflect my empty, isolated, pathetic state.

I often thought of Robert DeNiro as the young Godfather, tapping his head and saying to his neighbors and friends in Italian, "I will remember." *I too* would remember—both those who went out of their way to help me and those, like McAlevey, who did me wrong. I desperately wanted to feel the self-assurance of the Godfather, knowing before anyone that one day I would be in a position of power to pay back favors and wreak revenge. But my confidence-boosting classmates were scattered across the country and I had only my battered ego to rely upon.

Of course, in the part of my mind that wasn't feeling sorry for myself or panicking or plotting revenge, I knew how besieged these executives were with phone calls and letters from job seekers like me. Even if they were decent and ethical, they could not possibly extend themselves to all of us. So it was always a pleasant surprise when someone was genuinely friendly and helpful to me.

J. Todd Harris, a Stanford MBA who had traveled along this same route four years before me, stood out. No matter how many times I called him for advice, he was always friendly and patient. Unfortunately, niceness and power rarely seemed to go hand in hand. He was currently an independent producer, with office space provided to him in exchange for a first-look agreement with Davis Entertainment, John Davis's production company in Century City. He told me that after Stanford, he had worked as an assistant at a television production company. He then raised $150,000 in a limited partnership, mostly from classmates, to use as a fund with which to option screenplays and develop film projects. He paid himself a $39,000 salary, which, I was depressed to hear, was the most money he had ever earned.

Another particularly affable production executive was Harvey Shulman at Columbia Pictures, a young UCLA MBA who befriended me early on in the process. I met him at his office in the Thalberg Building on the former MGM studio lot in Culver City. As part of a $500 million legal settlement with Warner Brothers (derived from Columbia Pictures' inducing Peter Guber and Jon Peters to break their contract with Warner), Columbia had been forced to trade its half interest in the Burbank Studios, which it had shared with Warner, in exchange for the much smaller MGM lot owned by Warner. Columbia co-chairmen Peter Guber and Jon Peters were gleefully transforming the lot with Sony's money, and construction crews seemed to outnumber studio personnel (they would eventually spend over $100 million on the refurbishment).

Shulman got straight to the point. "I know exactly what you're going through. I went through the same exact experience after I got my MBA. So don't worry, it *can* be done if you hang in there and tough it out. Tenacity is everything. So, how long have you been doing this madness?"

I smiled, grateful that I didn't have to put on airs for him. "I began hitting the town several months before business school graduation, and it's been three months since I moved down to L.A. I just don't know how much more of this I can take."

"That's it? You gotta be kidding! I'm afraid that's really not a lot of time at all. You've gotta give it at least a year, maybe two or three. Hell, I know guys who have been looking for a creative executive position for the last four years. It's all a matter of persistence—that's all it is. And knowing the right people, of course."

"Four years! I think I'd sooner work as a bicycle messenger than wait four years for lightning to strike."

"I hate to break it to you, *bubbele,* but unless you're independently wealthy, you might have to consider a job like that. Have you considered temping?" No way. That would mean admitting that I wasn't going to be one of the "lucky ones" and immediately land an entry level creative job.

I shook my head. "No, first I want to see how my interviews with the studios play out. Plus, I don't think I can quite picture myself temping. Isn't all the typing and phone answering degrading?"

"You have no idea about degrading. I'll tell you degrading. I worked as assistant to Harry Roth, the producer. First, I once had to take a sample of his dog's shit and bring it to the vet for testing—I kid you not. Another time, Roth asked me to watch his sick dog over the weekend. Just my luck, that weekend the dog's condition deteriorates. He gets much sicker and dies. I had the pleasure of telling Roth on Monday morning that his beloved dog—his most prized possession in the world—was dead! I also have a friend who was a driver for Joel Silver. One day, he drives Silver to the Fox lot and by mistake overshoots the guard booth by a few feet and has to back up. Big deal, right? Silver was so embarrassed that he fired the kid on the spot."

I laughed with him. "I guess I have a while to go before I can really start complaining." I was right. Later on, I heard other assistant-abuse stories, like the television executive who returned to work from maternity leave and required her assistant to clean out her breast pump each day.

"Listen, the best advice that I can give you is to concentrate on getting the job...*any* job. You can always turn it down afterwards or work in it temporarily until something better comes along. Also, I get the feeling that you wear your MBA on your sleeve. Not a smart idea here. You've got to downplay the MBA. It'll only intimidate all the college dropouts in the industry who couldn't give two shits about what school you went to. The first place to start is to wear something a bit less Wall Street when you go to interviews and meetings."

"Geez, does it show that much?" I said, as if he'd just told me I had a bulbous growth on my forehead. I observed Shulman's stylish outfit: a fashionably wrinkled white shirt, Nicole Miller cartoon-decorated tie, and baggy pleated trousers. I looked down at my navy blue pinstripe suit, which I had bought on sale at Barney's in New York, and my red foulard tie from Abercrombie and Fitch. I had never given much thought to my wardrobe, and realized that I did not own any business clothes other than those from my Wall Street, junior investment banker days.

I took Shulman's advice the next day and drove to Fred Segal, the quintessentially hip L.A. men's store in Santa Monica. I wandered past an espresso bar and through a hodgepodge of different clothing-designer rooms where snooty salespeople eyed me suspiciously. They were hoping I'd leave soon so I wouldn't sully the image they were trying to achieve. One day, one day—bang-zoom! I lovingly fingered a black silk shirt and searched for the price tag, which was hidden under the label. If you gotta look, amigo, you can't afford it. $360—gulp. That quickly returned me to my original quest for a true Hollywood tie. I figured that my suit and shirts could pass as long as I had jazzier cravats.

I browsed among the rainbow of patterned Eurotrash ties that filled row after row of wooden display cases. As I selected what I considered to be several bold prints, a solicitous, balding salesman clad entirely in black rushed over, only now certain that I was indeed a cash-carrying customer. He was straight out of the Rodeo Drive shopping scene in *Pretty Woman*.

"Can I help you with something today?"

I tried the old standard. "No thanks, I'm just looking." He frowned but didn't move away.

"Have you seen our barracuda tie?" He bent over, moved his face within inches of mine, and looked me in the eyes. I stepped back.

"N-no, I haven't..."

He moved closer to me, conspiratorially, and whispered: "Just came in yesterday. From Europe. Very gorgeous. Very powerful. Very different..."

He showed me a blue tie covered with white barracudas.The largest one pointed aggressively to my zipper when I held it to my collar and looked in the mirror.

"That looks *fabulous* on you—*very* nice," he gushed. But no matter how I held it, I was wearing a fish. I put it down to his clear disapproval and selected two ties with large geometric patterns— very flashy for Wall Street but downright conservative for the Hollywood crowd.

CHAPTER 5

The Interviews

Show business is dog eat dog. It's worse than dog eat dog. It's dog doesn't return other dog's phone calls.

WOODY ALLEN IN *CRIMES AND MISDEMEANORS*

"**H**ave you got any coverage samples?" I was frequently asked during informational interviews. What, I wondered, was this mysterious coverage thing? More important, did it take any skill?

Coverage, I soon learned, was nothing more than a glorified book report, or *Monarch Notes,* for the busy production executive. It did take a certain amount of discipline to distill a 120-page script into a short sentence describing the premise (also called the "logline"). For example, *The Wizard of Oz* would become "Teenager in Kansas knocked unconscious during tornado whereupon, in a dream, she embarks on perilous journey to visit the Wizard who helps her return home." As you can see, it tended to reduce all stories to a *TV Guide* blurb. Screenplays that could be easily condensed into a provocative logline, however, were coveted by production executives and termed "high concept."

High concept, an overused term in the industry, described those screenplays whose two-sentence story idea alone was sufficient to hook audiences, regardless of casting, film reviews, or word of mouth. The term was attributed to Barry Diller, who as a programming executive at ABC in the seventies introduced the made-for-TV movie and with it the need for stories that could be marketed in 30-second spots. The ultimate in high concept was to invoke the title of a successful film. For instance, *Alien* was pitched as *"Jaws* on a spaceship."* And a slew of films had followed *Die Hard* as brand extensions: *Die Hard* on a battleship *(Under Siege)*, *Die Hard* on an airplane *(Passenger 57)*, *Die Hard* on a mountain *(Cliffhanger)*, and *Die Hard* on a bus *(Speed)*.

Coverage also included a one- to two-page synopsis of the story followed by a short critique of the screenplay's overall quality and commercial viability, as well as a judgment of the writer's talent. Coverage always ended with the words PASS or CONSIDER. (Theoretically there was also RECOMMEND, for scripts that needed little more than a polish before being sent to production. But unless you were a kamikaze reader, you'd be much safer with a CONSIDER.) If the script merited a CONSIDER, the executives then read it. However, if it received a PASS, it was usually impossible to rescue it from the reject pile.

One of the many ironies in film development was that these judgments were made by a lowly reader, often the entry level job on the creative side. Thus, a writer's career was held in balance by a twenty-four-year-old fresh out of college making $500 a week. Still, with over twenty-five thousand scripts registered each year with the Writers Guild, the coverage system was the only way production executives could give an individual look to the barrage of scripts arriving each week.

I reasoned that if I was eventually going to be reading coverage as a production executive, I had to demonstrate to myself that I could write it effectively. The problem was that the major studios only hired story analysts who were union members. (Yes, there was actually a union for story analysts: Local 854 of the International Alliance of Theatrical Stage Employees.) The Catch-22 was that you could only become a member of the union if you worked as a reader for at least thirty consecutive days at a unionized film company. The independent production companies did use freelance readers at $35 to $50 per script, but those jobs were nearly impossible to get. I therefore proposed to a TV production company story editor, whom I had befriended, that I do some coverage for her for free. She was all too happy to dump in my lap some of the many, mostly horrible, scripts she received each day. In this way, I also developed samples to show the executives when interviewing.

Good coverage would get you an interview, but your script notes determined whether you'd be hired. If coverage was an X-ray of the script, notes were surgery. Instead of focusing on a synopsis, notes assumed the reader was familiar with the script's plot and liked the basic premise of the story. Notes were addressed to the writer, advising him on what was deficient in the script and, most importantly, how to fix it. As Paramount instructed its creative executive candidates: "Your goal is to write a set of notes such that if the writer followed them to the letter, he would turn in a new draft to which you would immediately commit $15 million to go out and make. Your objective is to turn the script into a $100 million hit." Pretty heady stuff for an aspiring production executive.

The ultimate fantasy in Hollywood and the wet dream of all production executives was to discover a dark and psychological script about a prostitute who is wed by a rich businessman and then dumped back on the street, and metamorphose it through excellent script notes into a shmaltzy and breezy $400 million monster hit called *Pretty Woman*.

Disney was notorious for their control over writers via their development notes, and with good reason. They carried the notes idea to the nth degree. They ended their comments with a section in which they analyzed, page by page, what should be fixed or clarified. ("Pg. 62: Here Suzy finally reacts to Bart's attempts at seduction with tears. We like her anger, but crying seems a little overdone.") Disney creative executives were also advised to write in the "imperial we," as if representing the entire studio. It seemed that Disney's goal was to recast their scripts into one of a few proven formulas. Every detail and element was scrutinized until all spontaneity was driven from the process. The young production executives at Disney who analyzed scripts by the truckload were akin to financial analysts on Wall Street who crunched numbers on spreadsheets, and their task was almost as systematized and spiritless. It was this policy of scientific controls that had made Disney the kind of studio many in the industry rooted against. After a string of hits like *Pretty Woman, Ruthless People, Down and Out in Beverly Hills, Who Framed Roger Rabbit?* and *Three Men and a Baby,* it was a pleasure for many to see some of their films flopping. *An Innocent Man, Gross Anatomy,* and *Blaze* were three successive duds, and even *Dick Tracy,* which grossed over $110 million but cost over $50 million to make, was deemed a disappointment.

Disney's development department, however, was a logical place for me to concentrate my efforts at securing an interview. They ran the proverbial boot camp for fledgling production executives and had twenty-five creative executives divided among their three film divisions, Touchstone, Walt Disney, and Hollywood Pictures. Most crucial, they were willing to hire MBAs to these positions. That evoked the classic Groucho Marx dilemma: Any studio that would put many MBAs in creative posts was not the sort of place at which I'd like to work. I lost count of how many times I heard the so-called Disney maxim: "If you don't come to work Saturday, don't bother coming in on Sunday."

Using contacts, I secured an invitation to write notes on a sample script for Disney. I spent a weekend holed up in my apartment clad only in underwear, sporting a three-day beard and feeling like a crazed screenwriter. I drafted what I considered to be a damn good set of notes. Several weeks later, I was rewarded with the next step—a series of interviews with five Disney vice presidents.

My main preparation for the interviews consisted of anticipating the inevitable favorite-and-worst-movies question. The hard part was to remember all the film titles under the pressure of an interview. I converted my favorite-dramas list into an acronym, using the first letters of their titles, and sat in waiting rooms mouthing these nonsensical words: BAAD SCRMG, BAAD SCRMG, BAAD SCRMG. Then, when each of the interviewers asked me to name my favorites, I unhesitatingly spilled out the names of ten films: *Butch Cassidy and the Sundance Kid, Annie Hall, Apocalypse Now, Deliverance, The Sting, Chinatown, Rocky, Moonstruck,* and *The Graduate.* I made it seem like I was casually thinking aloud. I had other mnemonics for my favorite comedies and action/adventure films.

"I like your taste," the executive usually said. Yeah, like I picked some controversial films. I mean, I'd have to be out of my mind to pick *Attack of the Killer Tomatoes* or *Hiroshima, Mon Amour.*

While interviews in corporate America are about six times as long as the time spent waiting in the lobby, Hollywood interviews had an inverse ratio to waiting time. I usually waited a half hour for a ten-minute interview.

Aside from talking about my favorite films, I forcefully made a pitch for myself: "Let me tell you—I see almost every film out there, and I know all the players. I'm also friends with a lot of young writers and agents, and I'm a pretty good judge of material." I paused before my clincher. "I am positive that if you just give me the chance, I'd be one of the best creative executives on your team. It's the only job in the world that I could see myself doing right now." I practically grabbed them by their ties and screamed in their faces, "HIRE ME!" Several times during these interviews, I momentarily left my body and watched and listened to myself, and could not believe how aggressive I was being. I think I was starting to believe my rap. I knew I was exaggerating the extent of my industry contacts, but reasoned that my competitors were probably many degrees worse.

In the nail-biting days following the interviews, I tried to marshal as many people as I could to call these Disney executives and tell them what a swell guy I was. These "godfather calls" were crucial to getting a position at the studios. You had to create a buzz around your candidacy.

I must have succeeded, as I was invited to the final round. Three candidates, I was told, had been summoned to interview with David Hoberman, the head of Touchstone/Disney. (Touchstone was their adult-oriented movie division; the Disney name was reserved for light-hearted family fare. It would be foolhardy, after all, to tamper with a brand name that was equivalent to the *Good Housekeeping* seal.) Only one candidate would get the position—not bad odds, but if I lost, there was no prize for the runner-ups.

I sat in the waiting room outside of Hoberman's office, dismayed as I watched the first candidate laughing and joking with Hoberman as he departed. They seemed like best friends. When my turn came, I gave a satisfactory performance in the five minutes allotted to me. (How much can you say in five minutes?) In my paranoid state, I must admit that I was disheartened, though, to see a black guy sitting in the waiting room when I got out. I figured right then it was all over. I knew that at the time Disney had no black creative executives. And sure enough, I got dinged several days later. I felt embarrassed afterwards when I found out that it was the first candidate who had won the job after all.

During the next month, I went through a similarly protracted and painful interviewing process at Fox and Paramount. When those too ended unsuccessfully, I was hit with a strong bout of depression. It was brought on by my reading a blurb in *Variety* and the *Hollywood Reporter* about one of my classmates at Stanford who had become vice president of finance at a small film company. I called her to congratulate her, and she bragged of her fantastic position, complete with a six-figure salary and stock options. With false modesty, she kept saying things like "I don't believe I deserve this, but...," or "I'm sure they didn't mean it, but they said I was a key member of the executive team." She then advised me to abandon the creative end and find a financial position, as if she were now a veteran.

I felt that after nearly five months in L.A. and hundreds of phone conversations and meetings, I had nothing to show for the effort. I was severely depressed that week, sleeping until noon most days, falling back to watching TV whenever I couldn't bear to make another phone call and face certain rejection. I rarely went out except to pick up the *L.A. Times,* food, and the occasional video. I read a newspaper article that had a checklist of depression symptoms, and I ticked off every box.

The friends that I had out here could not be counted on for much comfort. My pals from business school who were living in Los Angeles, like Mitch, were so busy during the first few months of their new jobs that it was difficult to schedule anything with them. I also had many pseudo-friends, like the girls from USC I met on the plane or friends of friends I had been told to look up when I got to town. I would get together with these people for drinks or dinner, but in the absence of any common ground, such as school or work, we never progressed from acquaintance to friend.

And the frequent messages my father left on my answering machine did not improve my state of mind. As soon as I played back the tape and it rewound for thirty seconds, I knew it was him. I usually waited until I was in a relaxed state of mind before playing the tape back.

"How's my happy, happy son in sunny California doing? It's about 12:35 here on Wednesday afternoon, and I'm just sitting in the office having a little lunch—just a poppy bagel and cream cheese, a boysenberry yogurt, and a tangerine." He always had to provide context. A heavy sigh (from him, not me). "I was just thinking about you floating around out there in Los Angeles." Another sigh. "And I just hope you'll come to your senses soon and get the hell out of California back to your family and friends in New York who love you. You have to realize that when you leave the beaten path, you're asking for trouble. All the rest of your classmates—they're in place. They are in place in their jobs, in their marriages, in their *lives*. You, on the other hand, are floating around. You're floating around with every other Joe who never went to business school, or college for that matter."

Even without my father's constant intonations of doom, I was beginning to question all aspects of my search: creative versus business end, Hollywood versus a "straight" career, Los Angeles versus New York. What finally raised my spirits and returned me with fervor to my search were the conversations I had with classmates in conventional jobs. They already hated their jobs and complained to me, knowing I'd be a receptive ear. And when I heard of the tedium they were experiencing in their investment banking or management consulting jobs, I began to feel better about what I was doing. My days were at least unpredictable and full of hope. And if it all worked out, I would be doing exactly what I wanted to do. They were just treading water until they figured out what they *really* wanted.

My friend Neil, in particular, was a kindred spirit who had also flirted with making a foray into the entertainment industry after graduation. Curly-haired, pale, and bespectacled, he looked every bit the part of a wiry, Jewish writer-producer. Neil had even taken a week off during spring term to network at the Cannes Film Festival. He printed up business cards for a bogus film production company and was admitted to all the screenings and parties. And while I attended several undergraduate acting classes on the side while at Stanford (business requires acting skills, I rationalized), Neil took playwriting. It was all the more disconcerting, then, when Neil copped out and joined a small investment bank in New York. He didn't just turn his back on his creative side; he opted for the most conservative company imaginable—a place decorated with lithographs of ducks, hunting scenes, and sailing ships, where the directors all had a roman numeral or "Junior" appended to their surnames, and no one spoke above a murmur. Neil nonetheless burned with a passion that was not touched by his tedious job.

"Uhhhhhh," he'd moan to me. "I came in after ten this morning, I just took a three-hour lunch and even that wasn't long enough. I can't take this anymore. I can't take it! I've got to get out of here!" "What's so bad about a ten-to-five job with a three-hour lunch break that pays over a hundred grand a year?" Neil wasn't exactly finding a sympathetic shoulder to cry on. "What's so bad? What's so bad? I'm going nuts—that's what's so bad. I woke up this morning with a splitting headache because I dreaded coming in to work...I'm just so sick of this shit. I hate everyone here. I even hate the receptionist!"

I pictured a split screen showing me lying on the couch dressed in a T-shirt and underpants and Neil in a suit and tie sitting in a gray cubicle, slouched over his desk. We were both silent for a minute, the kind of silence that good friends allow in conversations without rushing to fill the void.

"I hate to admit it, Everett, but I think you were right after all. I mean, you're gonna make it in Hollywood if you hang in there long enough. I just hope you make it soon so you can rescue me from here."

"Hey, don't think it's such a picnic out here either," I said, though his comments made me feel better.

"Yeah, but at least you don't have to sit in meetings all day listening to lawyers argue about securities law."

"You definitely have a point there." But I was getting impatient with his constant complaining. "So what do you want me to say, Neil? Either go in there with an assault rifle tomorrow or quit already!" He was all talk and no action.

"But where will I go from here?" he wailed. That was the key question. His whining annoyed me, but also forced me to realize that the more ensconced he became in his perks, his high salary, and his cushy job, the harder it would become to make a bold, dramatic move. I might be a broke wannabe sitting in my underpants, but I was still alive and kicking. Neil was a drowning man. Until I could find an alternative career path that excited me as much as Hollywood,

I was determined to fight it out. If I didn't try this now, I'd never again have the guts.

I finally realized that lightning was not going to strike. My college roommate's stepfather was not returning my phone calls. My mother's cousin was actually not a big Hollywood producer—he owned a video store in Pasadena. And my meager attempts at interviewing for jobs were just that. Most important, I was swiftly running out of money and refused to ask my parents for help (okay, *more* help). Suddenly, the T-word didn't sound so farfetched. In fact, temping began to sound like my best option.

I had delayed the decision for weeks, unable to see myself answering phones and typing letters. But I was nearly broke. I had recently begun to view coupon clipping as a major source of revenue; the supermarkets in L.A., after all, gave double value to coupons. Then there were the forty-nine-cent frozen bean burritos—two of them cooked for one minute in the microwave was a nutritious dinner for a dollar. It was amazing how cheaply I could live after cutting out all discretionary purchases. However, it didn't make for fun living.

I finally relented and scheduled appointments with several temp agencies dedicated to the entertainment idustry. There were at least five of these in L.A.: Right Connections, Our Gang, Friedman, All Star, and London Temps. I was surprised to learn that all were booked several weeks in advance. Apparently, I was not the first to go this route.

Temp agencies and Hollywood go together like plastic surgeons and aging starlets. Studios love temps—they work for low wages, cost nothing in medical insurance and benefits, and can be hired and fired with ease. Young wannabes love temping in the industry because it's often their only opportunity to get a foot in the door and makes them feel like they're working full-time in Hollywood.

My first appointment was with the Right Connections agency. I arrived early and announced myself to the gum-chewing receptionist, who perfunctorily handed me a clipboard and told me to take a seat in the waiting room. I gloomily looked around at the polished, twenty-something candidates busily filling out the same forms I was holding: an employment history, plus a secretarial test with misspelled words, a filing quiz, and some basic arithmetic. Look, mom and dad, at what your son's doing now.

I zipped through the application and handed my clipboard in, pleased by the receptionist's surprised look at how quickly I had completed the forms. She led me to a small alcove with an electric typewriter and an egg timer. I had never taken a typing test, nor expected I would ever need to. My hands shook slightly as I raced to complete the test. Why don't they give these tests on computers? I scored a respectable sixty words per minute, but only forty-eight after all my mistakes. I should have paid more attention in high school typing class, but who knew?

I was eventually ushered in to meet the two matrons of the office, Harriet and Pauline, two blond, plump forty-year-olds who began talking before I had even crossed the threshold.

"So, why are you here?" "You've got a very impressive resumé. Very impressive."

"You should be on Wall Street or something with these qualifications." "Absolutely top-notch."

That's how they spoke. One would say something and the other would immediately paraphrase it. Their questions were mainly rhetorical, as they didn't bother waiting for answers.

"We should be able to get you out immediately." "Disney *loves* MBAs."

"Do you know who the players are in the industry? It's very important in this business to know who's who." "I hope you read the trades."

"Have you been shown the time sheet forms?" "We need to get the forms back by Wednesday in order for you to get paid that week."

I cleared my throat. They both stopped suddenly, aware that someone else was in the room.

"Do you have any questions, dear?"

With my bank account as close to zero as it had ever been, I sure did. "Yes, I do, actually," I said, nonchalantly, not wanting to appear anxious. "Just out of curiosity, exactly how much will I be making per hour?"

"It's not the money, it's the experience." "Who can put a price on contacts?"

I smiled. "Just humor me. How much?"

"Ten dollars an hour." "Plus time and a half for overtime."

Ouch. Even if I worked forty hours a week for fifty-two weeks straight, I would only make $20,800 a year pretax—less than a third of the average starting salary of my classmates.

I thought I'd drop my name at one agency and, "bidi-bing, bidi-boom," they'd lust over me, giving me my choice of jobs. Well, it turned out there was no dearth of highly skilled secretaries seeking employment, and I was considered overqualified. I was registered with five agencies, yet no one had called after two weeks.

That's when I started going a little nuts while waiting. If I hadn't been looking for a job, my life would have been a picture of what retirement would be like (albeit without Social Security). I was constantly going to movies, either with Mitch or alone, always able to justify it as work-related research. One weekday, I went to the AMC multiplex in the Century City mall. I began with *Presumed Innocent* at noon, followed by *The Two Jakes* and *Arachnophobia,* then parts of *Problem Child* and *Navy SEALs*. I exited at seven in the evening, feeling exhausted and slightly nauseated from seven hours of darkness and moving images.

I also exercised to improve my mood, figuring that endorphins were the only drug I could afford. I made the pilgrimage each day to the mecca of muscle, Gold's Gym in Venice. Where else could an average guy like me pump iron alongside huge, "highly ripped" freaks? I loved the place. It reminded me of Brooklyn—no matter whether these guys came from San Diego or St. Louis, they all tended to walk like Italian guys I grew up with. Except these guys had tans and were wearing tiger-striped baggy pants and magenta sweatshirts.

There was no valet parking, concierge desk, juice bar, or laundry service at Gold's as there was in the ultra-chic Sports Club L.A. Just the clank of weights, the smell of sweat, and a cacophony of heavy grunting sounds. This atmosphere, plus the professional bodybuilders and the pinups of Schwarzenegger on the walls, did much to inspire me. I was never in better shape, though I always felt anorexic in the gym.

I could never forget that this was L.A., as I invariably spotted celebrities there. But unlike on the city streets, at Gold's people went out of their way to be nonchalant and cavalier. "Oh yeah," they would say with disdain, "Gregory Hines—he's not so fuckin' big." Weight-lifting was one of life's equalizers.

Another apparently logical and profitable way of using my free time occurred to me: Hey, I'm in Los Angeles, I have tons of free time, I need spare cash, I'm an educated guy. Why not try out for all the TV game shows and make a small fortune?

I showed up with assorted characters from all over the United States at tryouts for *The Challengers, Joker's Wild, Monopoly, Jeopardy!,* and *Tic Tac Dough.* But once again, I was not the first person to think of this idea. Thousands of people called in each week for tryouts, and the producers of these shows needed to cull intelligent and colorful applicants from the masses. The first barrier was a written trivia test, a grab-bag of more or less useless information. ("Name the capital of Idaho." "A dodecagon has how many sides?")

Predictably, the *Jeopardy!* exam was the most difficult—it was probably twice as hard as the English section of the SAT. About a hundred wannabe contestants sat on wooden fold-up chairs in an empty soundstage in front of two large-screen TVs. Alex Trebek appeared on screen, and the tourist couple to my right actually squealed in excitement. "Welcome, contestant hopefuls, to this *Jeopardy!* tryout!" And then, quite rapidly, answers flashed on the screen, each one in the $1,000 level of difficulty. I stared in dismay as they flew by. In the category of British Royalty: "Henry VIII was her third husband, and she married again after he died." (Who was Catherine Parr?) In the category of Nineteenth-Century Women: "This abolitionist was born into slavery in New York, and the first language she spoke was Dutch." (Who was Sojourner Truth?) I failed miserably.

I did pass several of the easier shows' tests. That's when several of us were invited to stand in front of a producer and tell them about ourselves.

"Hi, everyone," said a guy in his fifties, wearing a kelly green sport coat, who looked like a larger version of Rush Limbaugh. "My name is Bob Henry Cooper Jr. I'm a taxidermist, and I was raised with my nine siblings on a livestock farm just outside of Des Moines, Iowa. That's God's country, you know! I've shaken hands with five U.S. presidents. In my spare time, I collect umbrellas—I have over four hundred different ones. I'm a member of the Sherlock Holmes Society, and I'm also an avid ham radio operator."

I was no match for the contestants from the Midwest. They were so damn eccentric that I felt like a wallflower in comparison.

Three weeks passed, and just when I felt my sanity taking leave, my luck turned. I was about to become a Hollywood power temp.

CHAPTER 6

Second Assistant

> *We must believe in luck. For how else can we explain
> the success of those we don't like?*
>
> JEAN COCTEAU

After the initial shock of waking up while it was still dark and quiet outside, I got dressed and reflected optimistically over my first temp assignment. I was to report to David Kirkpatrick, the head of production at Paramount, the epicenter of the creative world in Hollywood. I knew all about Kirkpatrick through the trades and had even written him a letter, though I never got back a response. Kirkpatrick had left Disney two months before and returned to Paramount as executive vice president of the motion picture group. He had joined Disney after quitting Weintraub Entertainment Group, the ailing independent film company that had released such bombs as *My Stepmother Is an Alien* and *Troop Beverly Hills*. He previously worked as production executive at Paramount for over eight years (the studio had sued him and Weintraub for breach of contract when he quit in early 1987).

I walked outside to my car with an upbeat feeling. I was dressed in my sharpest suit-and-tie combination. The air was cool and moist, and I had to turn on the wipers to clear the icy screen of dew from the windshield. The streets were deserted at six-thirty, though Santa Monica Boulevard was already busy, mostly with expensive imports racing by me at seventy miles per hour. I rolled down the window, and the cool air licked my face as the sun slowly rose on the horizon.

I pulled into the Paramount driveway on Melrose Avenue as a black Porsche ahead of me sailed through the famous ironwork gates, an outstretched palm waving out the driver's window. My turn now, and I lowered the radio volume and pulled alongside the guard booth. Seeing my beat-up Toyota, the gray-haired guard put down his cup of coffee, frowned, and leaned into my window.

"I'm temping here today," I said, trying to sound authoritative.

He pointed behind me. "Turn around and try to find parking on Van Ness."

"I'm working for David Kirkpatrick."

The guard immediately whirled, grabbed a clipboard, and had me sign in. He pressed a button and the gate flew open.

"Go straight and park anywhere in the main lot that's marked VISITORS."

Bingo, I was in! I was psyched and let out a yell. I had never been allowed to drive onto the lot when I worked in finance at the studio. I wondered if one day it would be me in that Porsche and the back of my palm that the guard saw each day.

I drove straight ahead and turned into a vast parking area that was dug six feet into the ground. (I learned that they sometimes filled this lot with water for ocean shots, as they did for the parting of the Red Sea scene in *The Ten Commandments*.) Ahead of me was a gargantuan billboard of a blue sky flecked with cottony clouds, more perfect in appearance than the sky above. As I searched for a spot, I could not believe the numbers of gleaming Porsches, Jaguars, and BMWs that lined the parking lot like Matchbox toys.

After maneuvering my cardboard windshield visor into place, I walked along the manicured path flanking the narrow studio street, which glistened from a freshly sprayed layer of water. Pruned ficus trees and flowers of all shades, in perennial bloom, decorated the paths. Honest to God—bluebirds and robins chirped and flew about. Paramount Studios was not merely another faceless corporate headquarters, but a movie set in itself.

The main administration building was a dowdy, cream-colored shack of a building, which made me all the more amazed at its modern air-conditioned interior. I guess senior management liked to hark back to the roots of the studio by keeping things simple on the outside.

207, 207—I listened for a minute and turned in the direction of the only sounds in the building. As I neared the office with a shaft of light spilling into the hallway, I heard an ingratiating voice.

"I'll FedEx them the scripts today, David. Your other callbacks from yesterday are—"

A clean-cut guy with short black hair, piercing brown eyes, and long sideburns paused in midsentence as I walked in.

"Have a seat, I'll be right with you," he said in a humorless, self-important tone. I sat down in the chair facing his, the desk console in between us.

"Mace Neufeld, Stanley Jaffe, Rosalie Swedlin, Bob Wachs, Howard Weitzman, Don Simpson," he tonelessly called out while looking at me, sizing me up.

My eyes immediately locked on the blue barracuda tie that dangled from his neck. Thank God I didn't listen to that salesman.

"I'll have your call list typed up in a minute, David."

The door to the inner office mysteriously shut without my noticing anyone touching the door. While I marveled at the electronic door closer, the assistant moved around the desk and placed the call book in front of me.

"I'm Brad Dorman, and you must be Everett from Right Connections." He was not introducing himself as much as stating the facts. "We have about fifteen minutes before it starts heating up, so I'll teach you the basics right now." He opened a spiral notebook in front of me and grabbed three colored highlighter pens. The left page was headed INCOMING, and the right side OUTGOING.

"Okay, our bread and butter—call list coding. As people call into the office, you'll mark the messages down on the INCOMING side. Then, a yellow highlight means we called the person back and we left word but they weren't in. A pink highlight means that person called back but David wasn't in. And a blue highlight means we called back successfully." He paused and flicked his eyes at the door to Kirkpatrick's office.

He began talking more rapidly. "Throughout the day, David will also yell to get so-and-so on the phone. We put those names down on the OUTGOING side. Those are calls he'd like to make." I tried to look like I understood, but Brad saw right through me. "Well, don't worry if you don't get it right away."

The door opened, and a voice bellowed, "Callbacks!" A worried look crossed Brad's face as he grabbed the book away and leapt to his seat.

"Trying Alan Greisman," he said. He murmured into the phone and a few seconds later shrieked, "Left word, trying Art Linson." Seconds later he again shouted, "Left word, trying Mace Neufeld." His nervousness was growing.

The voice ordered, "Give him some names too."

I guessed that I was "him." So much for my warm welcome to the Paramount family. Brad cautiously placed a list in front of me and whispered, "Dial these carefully."

I dialed the first, and an assistant answered, "Howard Koch's office."

"Is he in? I have David Kirkpatrick for him."

"Yes, he is."

"Hold on for David, please."

Brad heard what I was doing and bellowed, "Howard Koch, Line One!"

He looked at me. "Is Koch on the line?" I looked at Brad quizzically. "Is he on the phone?" he hissed.

"Goddammit!" the voice thundered from the office. A few seconds passed and the voice metamorphosed and became charming and friendly. "Hiii, Howard, how are you?"

But I knew I had screwed up. Brad leaned over the desk and stared into my eyes. "I forgot to tell you this. Never, *ever* pass David a call until you get the person on the phone. Only when you hear them say hello, then and only then do you pass it to David. He freaks out if he has to talk to the assistant."

I sensed a Catch-22. "But what if that person's assistant is also waiting for David to get on? Who gives in first?" I smiled.

Brad wrinkled his brow and frowned. "Don't worry about that. Only a few people get that treatment, like [Paramount Chairman] Frank Mancuso or Eddie Murphy, and I'll handle those calls. Now get ready again."

As Kirkpatrick hung up his phone, Brad shouted, "Trying Dave Gersh," and waved his hand at me.

"Trying Bernie Brillstein," I said, feeling stupid.

We worked the phones most of the morning. Most of what Brad and other executive assistants did all day was call maintenance: the constant typing and retyping of phone lists. It was the chronicle of a never-ending game of phone tag. The phone log itself also served as a valuable snapshot of one's business interests on a given day. (In fact, some production executives have had their phone logs subpoenaed for evidence in trials involving the studios.)

When not on the phone, Kirkpatrick carped constantly at Brad for not moving fast enough or moving too fast. Anything could set him off, and Brad was always on edge. I wasn't directly involved, because I didn't even exist in Kirkpatrick's purview. The bearded executive (beards seemed to be the rage in Hollywood, perhaps due to the influence of Steven Spielberg), who wore impeccably starched white shirts and smelled of expensive cologne, walked past me many times that day and didn't once acknowledge my presence.

As far as I could see, Kirkpatrick seemed to have no other life besides this job. He came in at around six-thirty each day and was at work until eight or nine at night, then usually off to a dinner meeting or a screening. Weekends were not sacred either, as that time was reserved for the infamous "weekend read" of the best scripts of the week (often five or more), which the creative team would discuss on Monday morning.

Even that first day I learned just how much of what production executives do is schmooze and gossip. "Tracking," it was sometimes called, or dialing all your contacts around town and trading secrets: who's doing what where and for how much. It was a tireless search for inside information. And Kirkpatrick worked the phones like a man possessed, juggling twenty different projects during the day.

Another big part of Kirkpatrick's job was casting the major roles for Paramount's upcoming movie projects. It was all about coming up with short lists of actors for given parts. In packaging a film, Kirkpatrick used the common Hollywood ratings system. Based on the input of his creative staff, he would write down "A-list" and "B-list" actors and actresses to play the male and female leads in a given film, and have Brad or me type it up. A-list actors were the top box office draws at that moment, or actors the studios wanted to champion (Arnold Schwarzenegger, Tom Cruise, Kevin Costner, Tom Hanks, Jack Nicholson, Mel Gibson, Harrison Ford, Michael Douglas, Eddie Murphy). A legitimate movie star was one who could "open" a movie, or generate big business during the crucial first weekend of a film's release. This allowed studios to trumpet the film's opening weekend grosses in double-page, full-color ads in *Daily Variety*.

Similar lists were made for directors and writers as well. These arbitrary rankings gave production executives like Kirkpatrick the ability to make or break careers, and it was not only excruciatingly difficult to break into these lists but tough to stay on, as you were only as good as your last movie.

It seemed to me to be a fun way to earn a living. Schmooze half the day, think up which actors should play a role, and enjoy two-hour lunches. From what I could see, Kirkpatrick, however, never seemed to enjoy himself at work. One of the coolest jobs in the world, wasted on someone who wouldn't or couldn't appreciate it.

Aside from answering phones that day, I was Brad and Dave's messenger boy. They dispatched me all over the lot to deliver Kirkpatrick's missives. Creative executives sent him memos, which he commented on in block capital letters. He'd write at the top "cc: FM, GL, KR, DG, TZ, KJ, MF, JK, DC, TB, BH," and I had to figure out which person the initials stood for and where everyone's office was. Still, it got me out of the office so I didn't have to make small talk with spooky, noncommunicative Brad.

I came home dog-tired that first night and quickly changed to a pair of shorts and T-shirt. I scanned the TV listings but couldn't find anything remotely interesting. It was definitely a video night.

At the Video Delight, I scanned the NEW ARRIVALS section. Not much of a selection—either it was a decent film and I had seen it in the theater, or it was trash and I would never see it in any format. I read movie reviews religiously and refused to see a film that was universally panned. But it also occurred to me that my principles might be putting me at a disadvantage. I kept thinking of Brad Dorman telling me, "I see *every* movie out there, good or bad." If he can do it, I certainly can too.

But I was concentrating mainly on the gorgeous green-eyed, button-nosed brunette dressed in strategically ripped and revealing jean shorts. I moved over to the rack she was looking at, desperately thinking of a line. I grabbed one of the most popular films in history, *Batman,* and asked, "Do you know if this is any good?"

She looked at me unblinkingly. "No, I haven't seen it yet." She was holding two John Hughes teen comedies in her hand. I'd always wondered who watched them. I groped for a response, as I hadn't counted on this.

"I hear it's pretty good. I guess a hundred million people couldn't be wrong." I smiled, figuring maybe she'd go for a certain amount of goofiness.

"Uh-huh..." But she was already moving down to the next rack. What an airhead. Still, maybe she was saying the same about me.

I finally selected two movies I had heard were particularly atrocious. Maybe they'd surprise me. Besides, selecting these kinds of films was going against my nature and was therefore therapeutic.

Later, I sat in bed, slice of Domino's pizza in hand, and fast-forwarded through most of the two videos. It was amazing how much you could skip of most Hollywood films and still follow the plot line. I forced myself to watch, though, pleased that I had found two new answers to the "Name some recent films you hated" interview question.

After several days, I developed a daily routine at Paramount and began to enjoy myself there. Phones with Brad until ten-ish. Script photocopying and mailing until noon. Lunch until one, followed by errands and more phone work the rest of the day.

I eventually became skilled at scheduling an errand across the lot immediately before or after lunch, knowing I'd finish the simple task quickly and be able to use the extra time to tour the lot. I assumed that the more I ventured out, the better chance something interesting would occur.

The big thing was to come back from lunch and matter-of-factly drop into the conversation the name of a celebrity you'd seen. "Almost got run over by Eddie Murphy and his Rolls Royce golf cart" or "Man, I had to wait five minutes for Goldie Hawn to read the memo and return it to me." It was important to be nonchalant and unimpressed, as if seeing the star were only tangential to the real point of the story. Brad was the king at this, only he'd never deign to tell me the stories. No, these he reserved for those waiting to see Kirkpatrick.

It chilled me to see Brad operate with these people. He was ingratiatingly effusive, and so consistent. He could tell the same anecdote or joke fourteen times in a row to consecutive guests. For the most influential guests, he acted as if he too were just visiting and, funny thing (ha, ha), just happened to be at the assistant's desk. Of course, he didn't *really* answer phones, photocopy, or do those menial tasks. He had me to do that. No, his mission was to chat up the guests and show off how "in the know" he was. If the ten o'clock appointment had said that Joe Blow was on the rise, Brad would conspiratorially tell the eleven o'clock appointment, "Well, it's obvious that Joe Blow is going places."

Snobbish and ingratiating, but I had to admit, Brad was a master. I couldn't even label the skill, it was so subtle. But like the famous saying regarding pornography, I knew it when I saw it. Still, I always sucked in my breath and dutifully did my tasks. Sometimes a guest would begin chatting with me. Just from reading the trades, I usually knew the guest's bio and most recent projects. I loved these moments: Brad Dorman watching with a baleful look as he realized that he'd been deprived of a moment in the spotlight. Miffed, he would return to work, probably assuming that any guest who preferred talking to me over him was a lost cause.

I must say, in Brad's defense, that this behavior seemed to be an occupational hazard. Certainly it was typical of the assistants in the other production executives' offices. Most assistants were women in their early 20's, attractive and polished, but also with little capacity for independent thought. I got to witness this firsthand on the occasions that we convened to celebrate someone's birthday. I invariably would be talking to some gorgeous blond named Kelly or Dana when somehow, like an Amazonian tribe that can immediately sense an intruder, they would hear me say something that threw them off and made them aware that I didn't belong. And I'm not talking about telling them that I was a temp. That was a word I'd long since learned to banish from my vocabulary, as it was the equivalent in Hollywood of saying you had an infectious disease. In fact, I thought I was sounding just like them, but their highly sensitive radar was picking up anarchistic signals from me.

Example of party conversation:

Me (spotting a beautiful assistant): Hi, I don't think we've met yet. I'm Everett, one of Kirkpatrick's assistants.

Kelly (unsure if she should be talking to me): Hi, I'm Kelly. I work for Teddy Zee down the hall.

Me (still flirting): Oh right, I thought you looked familiar.

Kelly (munching on carrot stick): You're new, right? You work with Brad, huh?

Me (pigging out on birthday cake): Yup, Brad and Dave—the dynamic duo. The Dave and Brad Show.

Kelly (already suspecting a subversive): You are *so* lucky—I hear Kirkpatrick always promotes assistants to development.

Me: Yeah, but you have to spend at least two years in purgatory first.

Kelly (almost certain I'm not one of Them): Still, they say everyone goes through this. Even Michael Eisner and Michael Ovitz were once assistants.

Me: Makes you think of fraternities and hazing, huh?

Kelly (now certain, frantically looking over my head): Uh, excuse me, I'm going to get some cake.

She then makes a beeline for the nearest group of chatting assistants.

One of the most frequent guests in the office was Don Granger, a twenty-six-year-old creative executive Kirkpatrick had brought with him from Disney and previously had brought to Disney from Weintraub Entertainment. Disney was actually suing Paramount over this, claiming Kirkpatrick was raiding their executives and stealing their film projects (Kirkpatrick's lawyer, Howard Weitzman, retorted in the *Los Angeles Times,* "Mouses that live in glass houses shouldn't call other people louses.") Granger, as far as I could see, functioned as Kirkpatrick's chief of staff, or hit man.

Granger would come bursting in, sweat beading on his forehead, his short-cropped, curly hair glistening with gel. He was a big guy, overweight by Hollywood standards, and yet wore baggy, double-breasted Italian linen suits, which made him look even heavier.

"Is he in?" he'd say, gasping for breath, his white shirt soaked with sweat.

"No, you just missed him," I'd tell him, smiling at his predictability.

"Damn!" He would then head to the window sill where Brad always kept a stash of cookies or pistachio nuts, which he offered to visitors. Granger would stand chewing with his mouth open, not a particularly pleasant sight before noon.

"When is that new office going to be ready?" I asked, knowing that Granger was irked that he was temporarily housed in a small office in a nearby building, oddly called Dressing Room.

"Any day now. I measured it; it's going to be at least fifty square feet bigger than any other creative executive's," he said with his mouth full. "Well, tell him I stopped by." And with that, he would rush back to his office, only to return in a half hour.

When all the creative executives came to Kirkpatrick's office for a schmooze session, usually at the end of the day, I had to bite my lip to prevent myself from laughing hysterically. This motley group showed up wearing designer eyeglasses and dressed in hyper-chic outfits, looking like a cast party for *The Revenge of the Nerds.*

Though I had spoken to many of them during the course of my job search, none of them would condescend to talk to an assistant as they walked by. While the coterie gathered around his desk,

Kirkpatrick smoked cigarettes histrionically, like a character out of a Bogart movie. I could see how important the head of production's vision was, for the production staff rarely contradicted his views. The meeting was typically eight people nodding their heads and laughing at his jokes, telling him what great ideas he had. It worried me that, try as I would, I found it difficult to picture myself standing there with them, unless I radically changed my personality.

My best source of gossip on all the creative executives was Rick in the photocopy center down the hall. With long, floppy brown hair, baseball cap, and aviator glasses, Rick looked more like a computer hacker than a photocopy machine operator. He was quick-witted and seemed way overqualified for his job.

"Hey, Rick, how's it going?" I said after several days on the lot. "Let me get ten copies, please." I handed him a script and leaned on the countertop, listening to strains of Wilson Phillips from his radio. "So, am I setting new records for longevity yet?"

"I think at two weeks you will. That's about when Kirkpatrick and his sidekick Brad conspire to make the ritual sacrifice." Rick expertly fed documents into the machine while filling out forms.

"Rick, what are you doing making copies? You should be running this joint."

"Hey, man, everyone tries to find a way in. My in happens to be the copy center. It could be worse, you know. I mean, I deal with all the muckey-mucks on the lot and read every single document that goes through these offices." He paused and considered whether to confide in me. "See, I'm also shooting my own film in my spare time, and the second it's finished, I'm gonna call in all my favors. Believe me, my aspiration in life is not to make fuckin' copies."

The fact that everyone working in the studios had a hidden agenda was one of the most pathetic aspects of Hollywood. It was at once hilarious and depressing. But with the excess demand for jobs and a supply of bright, ambitious people willing to do anything, even many "back office" jobs got filled with wannabes. Thus, virtually everyone, from the security guards to the cafeteria workers to the janitors, tried on the side to befriend the creative executives and show them a blockbuster script, pitch them a surefire story, or display star-caliber acting talents. It was the "no-brainer" aspect of Hollywood—the fact that most everyone in L.A. believed that they could do a better job than most of the studios' anointed executives, if only given the chance. Of course, this belief was reinforced by stories of the latest ex-hairdresser or tenth-grade dropout to land a multi-million-dollar production deal. The industry was like a prestigious university that was nearly impossible to gain admission to and yet ironically not very difficult once you got in.

One day, I was alone in the office when a dapper guy in his late thirties walked in. He was Armanied from head to toe; he wore a checkered sport coat with patterned shirt and tie. Unlike many who unsuccessfully attempted to look like a *GQ* layout, this guy looked like a runway model.

"Hi, can I help you?" I said. "Are you here to see David Kirkpatrick?"

"Yes and no." He immediately peered around into Kirkpatrick's office, checking to see if he was in. He looked back at me. "Mind if I sit down?" He made himself at home, dropping his briefcase and jacket on the adjacent chair. I just stared, amused and dumbfounded.

He handed me his card. "I'm Brian Melstein. Are you Kirkpatrick's assistant?"

"Yeah, sort of . . ." I read the card with puzzlement. He was an advertising account executive at Chiat/Day.

"Are you here to talk about an ad campaign with David?"

"No, actually I'm going door to door, making my rounds here in order to try and get in to see as many executives as possible." He pulled out his Filofax and Montblanc pen. "Let me get your name."

"It's Everett. But I assure you, I'm quite powerless here."

"Hey, you never know. One day you might be running this place."

"Don't tell me *you're* looking to break into this business. You've got a great job at the hottest ad agency in town."

"How'd you like to be working on the Q-Tips account for two

years, spending most of your time worrying if the cotton swabs have been photographed in the best light? I know, I know, it's going to take a lot more than just mailing resumés. But I've already met most of the creative executives here."

I smiled at him, sure now that he was slightly crazy. I considered calling security, but figured he was harmless and would leave soon enough.

Just then, Brad walked in. He sat at his desk and looked at Melstein as if he were an amoeba under a microscope. "Yes, can I help you?"

"I was just telling Everett that I'm trying to get an appointment to see David." He looked down at his notes. "You must be Brad Dorman right?" He smiled broadly and extended his hand. Brad ignored it, letting the guy's hand hang in the air until he awkwardly withdrew it.

Big mistake, fella. Even if you had a shot to win Brad over and get an appointment, you decimated those chances by invoking my name. You do not know the meaning of the word "territoriality" until you've stepped on Brad's turf.

"First of all, *I* handle all of Mr. Kirkpatrick's appointments. And second of all, if he doesn't know you, which I assume he doesn't, he won't see you. At best, you can leave a resumé with me, and then you'll have to leave." Ouch.

Melstein blanched and stood up, quickly retreating from his aggressive technique. "Hey, listen, I'm really sorry to bother you. I'll just leave you this for David and be on my way."

When he had left, Brad crumpled the resumé into a ball and threw it in the wastebasket. "We get that all the time. Don't give them any encouragement at all. David will flip out if he sees them in the office."

★

I relished the times when neither Brad nor Kirkpatrick was in the office and I could snoop to my heart's content. My favorite pastime was walking into Kirkpatrick's office—the inner sanctum. First, I'd grab a handful of his roasted almonds. Munching on them, I'd stand behind his glass-topped desk and peruse the few index cards with to-do lists, meticulously ordered. His office was immaculate—no drawers, no files, no books. It looked like it was about to be photographed for a *Vogue* layout. He seemed to be saying to the world, "I am totally on top of things. I don't need messy papers—the knowledge is all in my head" (most other top production executives were the same way).

I'd usually walk to the minifridge and taste the ever-present grapes and freshly baked cookies. The rule of thumb for these production executives was to live like Medicis and charge the expenses to the studio. The studio, after all, would eventually kick you out mercilessly, so you might as well take advantage of the system while you could. Talk about distorted incentives. No wonder overhead at the studio was impossible to cut.

The most enjoyable moment alone, however, came when I opened the secret door to use Kirkpatrick's executive throne room. This bathroom was a work of art. You'd never know it was there; its door blended with the paneled walls. Brad showed it to me once in awe. The accoutrements were particularly impressive: linen towels and terry washcloths, colognes, flowers (I had no idea when these flowers were replaced, as Kirkpatrick seemed to be in his office day and night). This was excess even Wall Street would find obscene.

Though I watched him in action twelve hours a day, Kirkpatrick was not the easiest guy to figure out. Like all production executives, he maintained an airtight facade of confidence, power, purpose. He rarely let down his guard. The pressure on him to turn things around at Paramount was enormous.

The studio had produced a string of franchise movie hits (also known as "tent poles," big-ticket films that spawned sequels capable of supporting less certain projects) in the eighties, like *Raiders of the Lost Ark, Crocodile Dundee, Star Trek,* and *Beverly Hills Cop,* all of which Paramount had milked with sequels galore. Most of these projects were developed when Barry Diller was the company's chairman, Michael Eisner headed the film division, and young Jeffrey Katzenberg ran production. This team left in 1984 for other studios. Since then the tent poles had fallen from overuse, and the studio was in a rut, desperately needing some new franchise films.

Paramount had seen its market share ranking fall from first place in 1987, with 20 percent of the box office, to fifth in 1989, with 14 percent. Thus far in 1990, Paramount had the surprise hit, *Ghost,* but had also produced such expensive bombs as *Days of Thunder* and *The Two Jakes.* Kirkpatrick was given the thankless job of leading this turnaround effort and was faced with the certainty that he could be fired at any moment. (To whit, a famous "inside" joke in Hollywood: Question: What's the last thing a production executive says to his secretary as he leaves the office for lunch? Answer: If my boss calls, get his name.) Adding to this pressure were the long lead times for projects—it would take from one to two years before Kirkpatrick's projects could be evaluated.

I learned more of him through his correspondence, which I filed on a regular basis. He was straight-to-the-point and seemingly emotionless in the voluminous notes he dispatched to his creative team through which he cancelled projects, slashed budgets, and bruised egos.

I read one letter written to him by a minion in the creative area at Disney asking him for an interview. In no uncertain terms, the junior production executive asked that Kirkpatrick keep the letter confidential for obvious reasons. Scribbled at the top in Kirkpatrick's unmistakable block capital letters was a note to Jeffrey Katzenberg of Disney: "JEFFREY, PLEASE MAKE SURE THAT YOUR EMPLOYEES DO NOT CONTACT ME AT PARAMOUNT. GIVEN THE CURRENT LEGAL PROCEEDINGS, I'M SURE YOU'LL AGREE THAT THIS IS BEST FOR BOTH PARTIES." I just kept picturing the poor schmuck who wrote the letter being called in to face an irate Katzenberg. Wow, *that* is heartless and Machiavellian.

Another applicant sent her resumé and letter to a Paramount senior production executive. Since she had formerly worked at Disney as well, the executive sent a memo to Kirkpatrick, asking if he recalled her. Again, in those menacing block capitals he scrawled: "THE GIRL WAS A PSYCHO. SHE HAD TO BE CARRIED OUT OF THE STUDIO ON A STRETCHER."

While Kirkpatrick went out for two-hour power lunches with agents or producers, on most days I stayed on the lot and ate at the studio commissary. I especially got a kick out of the guy who coordinated the kitchen area but looked and dressed like a stylish production executive. He spent half his time helping dish out meatloaf and potatoes and the other half networking. He probably was feverishly writing scripts on the side. Occasionally, he even wore the infamous barracuda tie.

Though I often ate with friends I knew from my summer stint in Home Video Finance, I sometimes enjoyed eating alone and reading the newspaper at the studio commissary. True, it was no classier than a high school cafeteria, but the movie posters showcasing Paramount's upcoming releases and the creative types running by made me aware that this was a Hollywood lunchroom.

One day a perky, petite redhead in her early thirties started up a conversation with me. When she heard I was working in Kirkpatrick's office, she immediately gave me a card on which was printed her name, the title "Script Consultant," and her phone number, and told me we should get together sometime soon. She held my hand and looked into my eyes a little longer than normal when we parted. I was beginning to realize the power some people associated with these assistant jobs.

During lunch hour or after work, I enjoyed exploring the sprawling sixty-acre studio lot, which was like a small town. I liked wandering around the back lot, peering into the movie soundstages, huge white structures shaped like airplane hangars. They were typically off limits with red light bulbs and forbidding signs marked CLOSED SET, but I could usually sneak in to look around. The guys who operated the Foley stages were amenable to visitors, and I often hung out and watched them work. Here, most sounds, other than dialogue, were added to a film after principal photography had been shot. (Jack Foley, for whom such stages are named, was an innovator of sound-creation techniques at Universal in the 1930s.) It was remarkable that these guys monkeying around in a dark room produced most of a film's incidental sounds. The film would be screened in front of them while the Foley artists ran around like maniacs, attempting to generate door knocks, pounding hooves, or rain storms. With every walking surface known to man spread about the floor in neat compartments, the Foley artists could re-create footsteps on gravel or marble or puddles or any other surface. Their ingenuity was impressive. Did you know that punching a watermelon produces a sound very close to that of a blow to the head? Or that walking on the unraveled tape from a cassette sounds like footsteps on grass? I didn't, and it was great to learn some of the tricks of filmmaking.

I sometimes stayed after work and walked to the back lot where the fake building sets were erected. My favorite was the New York street with its facades of brownstones, storefronts, and graffitied apartment buildings (the Hollywood version was far too clean and tidy). I liked to knock on the fake bricks as I walked by and hear the hollow wooden sound.

During the previous summer, when I worked at the studio crunching home-video numbers, I had spent a memorable evening on this street. I heard that Eddie Murphy was going to have a building blown up for *Harlem Nights,* which he was writing, directing, producing, and starring in (audiences later laughed when

Murphy's name appeared five times in the opening credits). On that night, I stood on the New York street with the cast and crew, who scurried about or simply waited as final preparations were made to the exterior of a 1930s-style Harlem jazz club. It became clear enough that we were waiting for Murphy to show up. That was business as usual: Movie sets tend to be boring places, with most of the day spent waiting for the stars to appear. It was like visiting the panda cage at the zoo.

After ninety minutes had passed, two golf carts came racing in. The lead cart stopped short, and Murphy, in his custom cart with the Rolls-Royce grill, rammed into it. It was like a Keystone Cops film, though no one dared laugh. Murphy and several obese bodyguards lumbered out and inspected the grill for scratches. He then stood on the sidelines with his arm around his date, a striking black model, while the assistant directors made the requisite last-minute checks. Finally, they cleared the area, Murphy yelled "ACTION," the two-story nightclub exploded with wood and shards of glass flying in the air, and that was it. Murphy joked loudly in an artsy voice, "Maurice, I don't think that I liked that take. Can we do that again?" The staff's laughter sounded a bit too hard and forced.

Like many stars, Murphy could cause studio executives to break out the champagne one day and the Maalox the next. He was a valuable box office property, but both his ego and his wallet seemed insatiable, as was revealed in the highly publicized trial that Paramount was embroiled in at the time. The case was based on Art Buchwald's claim that Paramount's *Coming to America,* whose story was credited to Eddie Murphy, was based on a two-and-a-half-page story treatment Buchwald wrote called *King for a Day.* Buchwald had proposed a story in which an African king visits the United States to purchase arms and is forced to live in a New York ghetto after he is overthrown. Producer Alain Bernheim optioned *King for a Day* and sold it in 1983 to Paramount as a potential vehicle for Murphy. Paramount later put the project in "turnaround."

Turnaround projects were those purchased and then abandoned

by the studio. Under Hollywood's code of law, the writer or producer could freely shop around a project in turnaround. The new buyer of the script would have to reimburse the previous owner for all prior development costs (including rewrites, interest, and overhead charges) plus a "rooting interest" in the project, typically 2 to 5 percent of net profits.

In the summer of 1988, Paramount released *Coming to America,* a film about the royal prince of Zamunda, a fictitious African country, who travels to New York and meets his bride in Queens. Buchwald and Bernheim recognized the story as an expanded version of *King for a Day* and sued Paramount. They won the case and were awarded the original fees stipulated in their story option contract: $250,000 and 19 percent of the net profits on the film. However, despite worldwide revenues of over $350 million, of which at least $125 million was paid to Paramount, there were no net profits to be distributed, as the film had actually lost money on the studio's books. In the subsequent ruling, now on appeal, concerning Paramount's accounting methods on the film, the judge awarded $150,000 to Buchwald and $750,000 to Bernheim.

Not that *Coming to America* was an especially egregious example of studio accounting practices; it was only one of the most closely investigated. Many of the top-grossing films each year showed net losses on studio books. Studios defended the practice of dumping expenses and overhead on highly profitable films by rationalizing that blockbusters had to subsidize flops.

Nonetheless, I was still surprised to learn that during the filming of *Coming to America,* Paramount spent nearly one-third of the film's $39 million on costs relating to Murphy, including his $8 million salary, his $200,000 writer's fee, and his $500,000 producer's fee. Approximately $1 million was spent solely on the salaries and living expenses of Murphy and his entourage (including $115,000 for his limousine and driver, $60,000 in travel and hotels for his staff, and $90,000 for his cost of living allowance, including a well-publicized $235.33 meal tab at McDonald's). The film was also charged $1.75

million for the costs of running Eddie Murphy's production company. One of Kirkpatrick's mandates in coming to Paramount was to better manage the Eddie Murphy relationship. When Kirkpatrick was an executive at Paramount in the early eighties, he had been the studio's direct liaison to Murphy. (Ironically, Kirkpatrick would later testify against Paramount in the Buchwald trial.) This relationship was not just a matter of star ego but much more about protecting a corporate asset. Since 1982, Murphy's film projects with Paramount had brought in over $1 billion in worldwide revenues. Still, it was hard to placate a star who was paid between $9 and $12 million up front per film against a guaranteed 15 percent of each picture's gross revenues, and yet publicly complained of being underpaid. This gross profit participation deal was the best a star could negotiate, for it meant a cut of every dollar the studio received from the film. And, since it was calculated from gross revenues, and not net, there was no opportunity for studio accountants to obscure the film's profits (as Buchwald learned). Net points were not only disdained by the Hollywood elite, they were mocked. Murphy was known to call them "monkey points."

Despite his considerable success in the 1980s, there was more recent evidence that Murphy's prima donna persona had become apparent to audiences. The image he had cultivated as a happy-go-lucky, cocky but endearing kid from the ghetto was now perceived by movie audiences and studio executives as increasingly arrogant. His reclusiveness and ever-present henchmen, coupled with unspectacular films like *Boomerang, The Distinguished Gentleman,* and *Beverly Hills Cop 3,* helped spiral his career downward. Finally, in the spring of 1994, Murphy took the route of other fading movie stars and switched agencies, from ICM to CAA. CAA promised to reshape his career by assigning four agents to him (including chairman Michael Ovitz and president Ron Meyer) and giving him full access to CAA's powerful client base of directors and writers.

One couldn't blame Murphy alone for Hollywood's out-of-control spending habits. I read some of Paramount's contracts with top stars and was astonished by the entourages they successfully demanded be included in the films' budgets: secretaries, chauffeurs, hairdressers, makeup specialists, nannies, acting coaches, masseurs, personal trainers. Contracts also stipulated the number of round-trip first-class plane tickets allotted to the star during the film's production. You would think that actors paid upwards of $5 million for one film could spring for some of their personal expenses! It was no wonder that the average "negative cost" per studio film (the cost of producing a finished negative, not including print-making, marketing, and advertising expenses) was currently $30 million and climbing.

Another visible sign of excess on the Paramount lot was the offices of producers Don Simpson and Jerry Bruckheimer, which occupied a small building in a prime location in the front of the lot. Overhead for these offices was rumored to be over $3 million. Often parked in front of these offices were the producers' matching black Ferrari Testarosas.

Early in 1990, the duo had signed a five-year contract in which Paramount would commit over $300 million to finance the production and promotion of five films, with the two producers receiving hefty profit participations. (Simpson had modestly summed the deal up in the *New York Times* by saying, "They put up the money, we put up the talent and we all meet at the theater." The two had also insisted that Paramount pay for full-page newspaper ads trumpeting their "visionary alliance.") Why had Paramount lavished so much money on two men who hadn't made a film in three years? Simpson and Bruckheimer had produced *Top Gun, Flashdance,* and the two *Beverly Hills Cop* movies. Their films had cost a reported $122 million and had earned over $725 million in the United States and Canada alone. Plus, Paramount sorely wanted to distribute two of the producers' upcoming films, *Days of Thunder* with Tom Cruise and *Beverly Hills Cop 3* with Eddie Murphy.

And yet, one year after the contract was signed and with only one film produced under the contract, *Days of Thunder,* Paramount terminated the agreement with the producers. I had seen memos flying back and forth between Kirkpatrick and Simpson-Bruckheimer Productions regarding disagreements over costs. After spending over $60 million on the less-than mediocre film about car racing, there now seemed to be a limit to the excesses that even Paramount would tolerate in the more temperate nineties. The pair reemerged one year later somewhat chastened and with a film deal at the frugal Disney studio, of all places.

Don't imagine, however, that drastic changes are in store for Hollywood. In the summer of 1993, Paramount rewarded the principal players responsible for the success of *The Firm* with a bonus. The studio bought new $100,000 Mercedes 500 SLs for each of Tom Cruise, director Sydney Pollack, and producers Scott Rudin and Jon Davis. This after paying each millions in salaries with generous gross profit participations. The head of production at Paramount, Sherry Lansing, explained: "We felt that when people go that extra distance, they deserve a pat on the back." The studio did learn its lesson from the ensuing negative publicity. One year later, Paramount rewarded the four principals involved in *Forrest Gump,* but this time chose the more modest Apple Powerbook computer as gifts.

Like Simpson and Bruckheimer, I too should have seen the end coming for me at Paramount. After more than two weeks on the job, relations between Brad and me had not progressed. I gave him none of the respect and adulation he craved from the second assistant. He let me know in no uncertain terms that the permanent second assistant would most likely be young, female, and drop-dead gorgeous—no one he felt might be competition for him. After all, Brad had been working for Kirkpatrick for less than two months and was still insecure about their relationship. He knew that if he kept Kirkpatrick happy, and if Kirkpatrick stayed in power, he had a chance to be promoted to creative executive. Margaret French, Kirkpatrick's former assistant, had recently been awarded a creative executive post, so there was precedent.

I had completed my round of errands that morning, running and sweating all over the lot distributing Kirkpatrick's memos, which were too important to wait for interoffice mail and had to be dispatched immediately. When I got back, Granger was in Kirkpatrick's office.

I had some free time and volunteered to organize and label Kirkpatrick's sizable script collection. Paramount at any one time had 150 to 200 scripts in various stages of development, not to mention projects in turnaround.

With black marker in hand, Brad elaborately showed me how to squeeze the script and write the title on the spine in block letters. Real brain-surgery-type stuff. As I wrote titles and then alphabetized the scripts, I chuckled as I recalled that rumor had it that producer Scott Rudin had hired a production executive based primarily on his ability to organize Rudin's script collection.

While working, I asked Brad about Paramount's latest hot script, which was about to go into production. "Hey, Brad, I just read *Dead Again*. What did you think of it?" I was curious, as I had disliked the script about a murdered concert pianist who is reincarnated, finding it to be predictable Hollywood gobbledygook with gaping holes in the plot.

He looked up, and hesitated as he thought of the appropriate response. "I thought it was a great script. Excellent plotting, good writing, surprise ending. It's going to make a great vehicle for Emma Thompson and Kenneth Branagh."

I smiled, for I had heard Kirkpatrick use nearly the same words the day before in a conversation with an agent. Suddenly, books slammed loudly on the desk inside Kirkpatrick's office. "I don't fucking believe this!" Kirkpatrick thundered. "Goddammit! Brad, Brad? Did he deliver the memos today?"

Brad turned to me with an accusatory look. "Did you do the daily run?"

"I heard him, Brad!" I snapped, annoyed that Kirkpatrick still didn't talk directly to me. "Of course I did."

Brad ran into the office, the magical door closed, and he came out after thirty seconds of muffled yelling.

"He says that Granger didn't get today's memo."

I still had the original with Brad's instructions, a Post-It on which he had written the initials of those who should receive it.

"Uh, Brad...DG is not on the list."

Brad frowned and grabbed the sheet. "Well, you should know by now that Granger gets the weekly production schedule memo." With fifteen different memos a day, I was supposed to guess which executives got which on any given day!

As Kirkpatrick continued to fume inside, Granger meekly walked out, and to his credit, he looked embarrassed.

"Hey, sorry, man. I didn't know he'd go off like that. Otherwise, I'd never have told him I didn't get a copy of the memo...It wasn't like it was a crucial memo either. Don't worry, though, I'll talk to him later when he calms down."

Later in the morning, Kirkpatrick was returning calls. "Get Nicita on the phone!" he shouted.

Brad sat there. Lately, he'd begun letting me do all the dialing, as if he'd promoted himself to supervisor. I dialed Wally Nicita, a producer on the Paramount lot whom Kirkpatrick had been calling frequently the past few days. She and her partner Lauren Lloyd were two of the few female producers in the industry, and together they had produced the moderately successful *Mermaids* with Cher.

I cautiously made sure she was on the phone.

"Wally, hold for David Kirkpatrick, please." Putting her on hold, I shouted, "I have Wally Nicita on line one!"

"WALLY Nicita?" Kirkpatrick screamed. "WALLY Nicita? I wanted RICK Nicita. RICK Nicita—not WALLY Nicita!"

Brad peered at me nervously. Even he seemed scared. He rushed into Kirkpatrick's office.

"What the hell is he trying to do to me? What the fuck is this? Things are *totally* out of control here... I can't handle this. I cannot deal with this, Brad. Not now. NOT EVER!"

While Kirkpatrick continued his tantrum, I had the woman on hold. I smiled and picked up her line. I felt oddly in control and superior to the hysterical display that was taking place in front of me.

"Wally, I'm sorry, but I was mistaken. David jumped on two other calls before I could transfer."

"No problem, hon," she said graciously. "Just have him call me later, anyway."

I put down the phone and smiled, as Kirkpatrick was still bellowing.

"Is he really serious?" I asked Brad, giggling nervously. "How the hell should I have known he wanted Rick Nicita and not Wally?"

Brad shrugged as the oak door swung shut.

"Who is Rick Nicita, anyway? I've never even heard of him. He's never called Kirkpatrick since I've been here."

"He's a very big agent at CAA," he snapped. "You should know who he is."

I went to lunch and returned to find Brad sitting at his desk with a dour look. I felt like a student about to get detention.

I put my newspaper down on the desk and sat down. "Is David still pissed?"

"Yes, David is *very* angry. In fact, he doesn't want you to return from lunch."

I jumped to my feet. I was stunned and began to tremble slightly. "W-what? You're fucking kidding, right? This is a joke...Tell me you're joking."

"No, it's not a joke. I've never seen him this angry before."

"After that one little mistake on the phone? Was that it?"

"Actually, it was a lot of things together. The missing memo and then the Nicita fiasco. And you've been taking a lot of time delivering memos lately." He shrugged. "Things are just not working out."

It suddenly dawned on me that perhaps innocent Brad was not entirely unhappy to see me leave and might even have played some role in my demise. I began to bristle with righteous anger.

"This is so screwed up. I've been coming in at seven every morning, staying until eight or nine, running around the lot for you and him. I think I've done a great job—just ask the other creative executives. I made two tiny mistakes that weren't even my fault. Well, let me tell you something..." I swallowed. I was so angry I could barely get the words out. "If you can't keep someone as good as I was, someone as qualified as I am, in this job, you can't keep anyone. This really sucks—it's...it's bullshit!" I would have liked to leave with a stinging indictment of Brad and his ilk, but I was too angry to be eloquent.

I left the office and walked down the hall in shock, pausing at the photocopy center.

"Well, Rick, they finally got me," I said with a lump in my throat.

"What?!" He stopped feeding pages into the machine and came to the counter.

"I just got the ax by Kirkpatrick for getting the wrong person on the phone. He didn't even have the guts to do it himself...Had Brad do the dirty work."

"That's rough, man. Just like the last few temps, too. Don't take it personally—it happens to the best. And you lasted the longest...Well anyway, stay in touch."

★

I was shaking as I drove home in the bright midday sun. I had never before been unsuccessful in a job, let alone fired. And without the second chance you were always supposed to get in life to improve. I really believed that I had been doing an excellent job, barring today's errors. Brad, however, had insulated me from Kirkpatrick, who had yet to even recognize my presence. It is pretty easy to fire someone you barely know; it's like dehumanizing someone, so it becomes easier to kill him.

In commiserating with friends in the industry, I soon realized that my experience was merely average on the abuse scale. Most young executives had experienced the same or worse while working under various monsters and screamers in Hollywood. Just talk to anyone who has worked for producers Joel Silver or Scott Rudin.

Rudin, for example, was perhaps the most infamous among film executives for the turnover rate among his assistants. It seemed like every other young Jewish male executive I talked to had at one time worked for him. In a cover story on Rudin, the *New York Times Magazine* recounted a story, denied by Rudin, in which he discovered that an assistant had forgotten to type one of his messages on the phone log. Rudin, it was said, called the hapless assistant into his office, held out his hands like scales, and said, "Six million Jews in the Holocaust. A message left off my log. I'd say they're about the same."

For weeks after I was fired, I effected my own kind of revenge on Brad. I would call Kirkpatrick's office at the height of the morning call-return routine just to hear Brad Dorman's voice feebly saying, "Hello? Hello? Hello! Hello!" I knew it pissed him off, disrupted his callbacks, and aroused Kirkpatrick's anger. Childish but satisfying.

Kirkpatrick's reign at Paramount was short-lived, demonstrating that the average tenure of a studio chief is often the same as the life span of a fruit fly. Shortly after I was fired, he became co-president of the motion picture group, replacing Sid Ganis, whom he was originally reporting to. (I had seen him edging out Ganis while I was there. It was as simple as excluding him from meetings or not sending him memos.) After producer Stanley Jaffe was named president and chief operating officer at Paramount in 1991, Kirkpatrick's days were numbered. Brandon Tartikoff, former head of programming at NBC, replaced Frank Mancuso as chairman of the motion picture group, and Tartikoff replaced Kirkpatrick with John Goldwyn, formerly of MGM-Pathé. Eventually, Tartikoff too was forced out—he lasted a year and a half—and was replaced by Sherry Lansing, Stanley Jaffe's longtime producing partner. Jaffe, in turn, would be fired following Viacom's acquisition of Paramount. (Did you get all that?!)

Following the route of many axed production executives, Kirkpatrick made a deal with Paramount and went "indie-prod" (the industry euphemism for getting pushed out by a studio and obtaining a lucrative independent production contract). He was rewarded with a three-year deal that featured a yearly guaranteed salary beginning at $500,000 (against producer fees per picture), profit participations on his films, and a budget that included $200,000 per year for development and secretarial staff, $250,000 for development expenses, as well as a furnished office and a car allowance.

Kirkpatrick's eighteen-year relationship with Paramount was finally severed when he was ousted from the studio in November 1993. Within a week, he launched a complaint in Los Angeles Superior Court, charging fraud, infliction of emotional distress, and breach of implied contract. He claimed that two days after he received notice, the company put his furniture out on the lawn. He further alleged that Jaffe had a personal vendetta against him and had refused to green-light any of his projects. Maybe, maybe not, but certainly Jaffe was no angel. According to press reports, Jaffe once yelled so hard at his staff during a divisional meeting that his nose began to bleed.

And so it goes.

CHAPTER 7

Prince's Nutritionist

The allurement that women hold out to men is precisely the allurement that Cape Hatteras holds out to sailors: They are enormously dangerous and hence enormously fascinating.

H. L. MENCKEN

Anton, my Belgian friend, drove up in front of my apartment building one balmy evening in October, and I climbed into his immense red 1969 Cadillac convertible. I found it amusing that the Europeans who lived in the States were fascinated by the muscle cars of the fifties and sixties. To them, the sheer massiveness and wastefulness of all the chrome and steel symbolized America.

I met Anton at business school and instantly took a liking to him, as we shared the same cynical outlook toward school and life. We both maintained a healthy sense of skepticism about the true amount of knowledge we would retain from our MBA. Anton, like many of the European and Japanese students, spent most of his free time at Stanford perfecting his golf game, hot-tubbing, and drinking beer.

Foreign students seemed to believe that the social networking aspect of the business program was far more important than statistics or options theory. I tended to agree with them.

Anton had recently moved to L.A. to begin working as a management consultant for McKinsey. He had spent most of the summer traveling throughout Asia, courtesy of a generous signing bonus. The postcards he sent me in the summer (usually of bikinied natives) were stinging reminders of the different path I had taken.

Anton was, as usual, a half hour late and in a mischievous mood. I often wondered if he was so cocky because he was successful, or successful because he was cocky. Either way, his blend of arrogance and elitism was infectious and uplifting in small, measured doses.

Anton pushed down his Ray-Ban Wayfarers, peered at me, and grinned from ear to ear. He was balding but had gelled his hair back, which made him look slick rather than nerdy. He was dressed in a white dress shirt buttoned all the way up, a navy blazer, faded ripped jeans, and black loafers without socks. All standard issue for the Eurocrowd.

"Hey, dude, looking pretty sharp," he said in his accent, which made him sound like Jean-Claude Van Damme.

I shook his hand. "Hey, stranger—welcome back! I see consulting life isn't treating you too badly either."

He peeled away from the curb—he loved doing that. Somehow the world seemed simpler when I was with him. You either were hip and happening or one of the millions of nonentities who colonized the rest of the world. I was flattered that he considered me worth taking along for the ride. The warm air rushed through the car as we followed the flow of traffic, and my problems seemed to recede somewhat.

"Tell me," he said, "If you're such the Hollywood type, how come I'm the one always finding the cool parties?" Anton socialized mainly with artistic types, preferably fellow Europeans, when he was in town and not traveling on a consulting assignment. He was one of the few people I knew who was happy *not* to be in the movie industry. More than once he had told me that he had the best of both worlds: He got the benefits of being around cool and pretty people at night but was spared the misery of dealing with the movie people during the workday.

"I keep telling you," I replied, "I don't want to be seen with you at the *really* hip parties."

"So, how is your assistant Jordan doing?" Anton and I shared a running joke. He and I pictured myself in ten years as this horrible, fat, lecherous producer who has a houseboy named Jordan. We constantly embellished this description with great delight. It was our way of making fun of the industry and the stereotypical movie executives.

"He spent an hour today waxing my back hair."

"That's right, that's right," Anton said, laughing hard as he pictured it and swerved to avoid hitting the black BMW in front of us with tinted windows and ultra-loud rap music booming out of it. I slumped down in my seat in case the Beemer's passengers fired at us with an assault rifle, the current rage in L.A.

Anton didn't blink an eye. "Jordan secretly loves you and you abuse the shit out of him. 'Oh Jordan, have you finished scraping my feet calluses?'"

"And the more I abuse him, the more he loves me. I'm the only guy he wants, but I'll never touch him."

We were driving down Santa Monica Boulevard, the wind blowing our hair back, laughing like madmen. I was having fun and wished we didn't have to go hang out in another loud club.

"And you only eat yellow M&Ms—no other color, just the yellow ones. You nearly took Jordan's head off when you spotted another color in your candy dish. 'Jordan, where the hell did this green one come from?'"

"And did I mention, I never wear underwear..."

"That's right, that's right. You put baby powder between your fat thighs because they always chafe. And—" He couldn't continue he was laughing so hard.

"What, what?" I said, not wanting to stop as we were on a roll. "You had a printer print toilet paper with hundred-dollar bills on the sheets just so you could say that you wipe your ass with money. And you wear these beige linen trousers that get really sweaty, smelly, and wrinkled."

"Right! And I throw them away after wearing them once. It's an idiosyncrasy of mine."

"No...no..." Anton was convulsing, and I wondered whether it was safe for him to be driving. "Every few weeks, you donate your used pants to charity. It makes you feel incredibly altruistic, and you brag about it to all your friends."

Tears were coming out of my eyes. "And I don't wear socks either. I wear these sandal-type brown Italian loafers."

"Right. And a humongous gold Jewish star."

We were still chuckling and wiping our eyes as we arrived at our destination in Venice. Anton expertly maneuvered the Caddy into a tight spot—he was an amazing parker. This club had no name, just an entrance in an alley. You'd never know anything was there except for the huge bouncers standing outside and the small crowd clustered in front of the door. Anton always knew of clubs like this, which only the fashion vanguard knew about. In fact, sometimes he got to these places and no one was there—he was *ahead* of the vanguard! Anton was on the cusp of nearly every new trend. He had his apartment in Manhattan Beach decorated in Southwestern motif before anyone else (all pastel pinks and greens with steer bones strewn about), and had moved on when it became the rage.

"*Salut, vieux,*" Anton said to the frowning bouncer in sunglasses at the door, ignoring the long, now hostile, line in front.

"Anton!" the bouncer exclaimed, a broad smile appearing on his unshaven face. "*Ca va?*" He unhooked the velvet rope, and we strode right in and paid the $15 admission.

The roaring techno-beat assaulted us as we stepped into the dark, throbbing room. He immediately spotted some French friends and ran over to double-kiss them. With him it was fend for yourself, unless of course you met a gorgeous woman, in which case he would magically reappear. I sipped on a Coors Light and watched people dance. I noticed a pale woman dressed in black spandex standing near me, swaying to the music. Kind of a modern version of Morticia Addams. She was wearing a huge silver necklace with a large African-looking wooden medallion.

"Where did you get the necklace?" I leaned over and said in her ear.

"WHAT?" she shouted over the roar of M. C. Hammer's "U Can't Touch This."

I motioned her to the back end of the bar and repeated the question.

"It was a gift from my boss. Do you want to dance?" So much for deep conversation.

We made our way through the crowd to the center of the small dance floor, where we had about one square foot of dancing space. Still, I was dancing, so the cover charge would not be a total loss. I scanned the bar for Anton, hoping he'd see me.

"WHAT'S YOUR NAME?" I shouted. She seemed oblivious to the fact that she was dancing with someone, but I forged ahead.

"KAT...IT'S SHORT FOR KATIANA." We danced some more, but no corresponding inquiry was forthcoming.

"MY NAME'S EVERETT...WHAT DO YOU DO?" I was really pushing my luck.

"I'M PRINCE'S NUTRITIONIST." We danced in silence for a few minutes as I absorbed that fact. I loved it. Prince's nutritionist. Clear, descriptive, matter-of-fact.

"YOU COOK FOR PRINCE?" I had to clarify this a bit.

"NO—HE HAS A COOK TOO."

"SO YOU PLAN HIS MEALS AND DIET?" I was fascinated, and she knew it.

"SORT OF—ACTUALLY IT'S A LITTLE MORE COMPLICATED THAN THAT." Yeah, right! I think I can handle it.

"SO, I BET EVERYONE ASKS YOU THIS—WHAT DOES PRINCE

EAT? I BET HE EATS A LOT OF GREASY MEAT AND CHEESE WHIZ."

She stared at me dumbfounded and continued to dance.

"NO, ACTUALLY HE'S A VEGETARIAN. I AM TOO." I don't think the women in L.A. appreciate my humor. Just a possibility.

"ARE YOU A VEGETARIAN FOR HEALTH OR HUMANE REASONS?"

"BOTH." She leaned forward and looked me in the eyes. I liked that. It made me feel like we were together and not complete strangers. "YOU KNOW THE AVERAGE AMERICAN EATS OVER FIFTEEN POUNDS OF FAT EACH YEAR."

"I DID NOT KNOW THAT," I said, feeling like Johnny Carson. As I contemplated that tasteful image, she looked around at the crowd by the bar.

"LISTEN, I'M GOING TO THE LADIES' ROOM. I'LL BE RIGHT BACK." Uh-huh, care to place a bet on that? I watched as she headed straight to the bar, kissed several people on the cheek, and joined them in conversation.

"She's pretty hot, dude." Anton appeared and put his hand on my shoulder as we both watched her.

"Does she look like she's headed to the bathroom? I don't think so."

"Look at all the talent here—goddam!" He wasn't lying. These women were unbelievable: perfect faces, taut bodies, full breasts. It was as if they were bred for these qualities. The songs and lore describing the women in Los Angeles were actually understated.

"The best bodies modern surgery can buy."

The evening's cover charge had been amortized, as I did leave with one phone number scribbled on a cocktail napkin: a cute woman with short blond hair and blue eyes in her late twenties named Deirdre who had spoken to me for ten minutes and had to leave early but was amenable to meet for a drink sometime. Deirdre was a "D-girl," as the female development assistants were known, at a small film production company in West L.A.

I waited two days before calling her so as not to appear over-anxious. We met at DC3, a chi-chi restaurant overlooking the Santa Monica Airport. I was relieved to see that she looked as good as I remembered her looking the other night. She was wearing tight black jeans and boots, a white spandex top, and a short, black matador-style jacket.

We sat at the circular bar and ordered drinks and appetizers. I turned to her, put my hand around her bar stool, and smiled.

"Now, where were we the other night?" I said.

She immediately went for the jugular. "So, you would never marry someone like me who wasn't Jewish, right?"

I looked at her with my mouth agape. "Whoa! Slow down there. I think we should at least complete our first date before we plan the wedding."

"I'm serious. Would you or wouldn't you marry a non-Jew?"

"I know you're serious—that's what's scary!"

She was unplacated and folded her arms.

"Deirdre, do you have some kind of experience in this matter?"

"Let's just say that I've dated a few of you Jewish guys before, and I went the distance with one guy only to see it broken up after we got engaged. I'm twenty-eight years old, and I don't want to go through that again."

I tried humor again. "Wouldn't you rather ask me the standard questions like what college I went to, whether I believe in an afterlife, what I thought of the crisis in the Persian Gulf?"

She sneered. "You guys are all the same. *Shiksas* are JFP—just for practice, right? Why won't you answer my question?"

I was becoming exasperated and approaching the point where I didn't care about avoiding the subject. "Well, if you want to know the truth, no, I probably wouldn't marry a non-Jewish woman."

She smiled with satisfaction. "I knew it! You Jewish guys are all the same. It's your parents, right?" She was hot stuff.

"Yeah, but it's not exactly like me coming home with a bad report card. It would destroy my family. My father would probably never speak to me again. *I* wouldn't want that either."

She mulled that over as she drained her vodka tonic.

The appetizers arrived, and I tried for a diversion. "Wow! Just look at those beautiful grilled vegetables!"

She speared a mushroom and slowly chewed while wrinkling her brow. "Well, what if the girl converted?"

I paused to consider that option. "That would be better. But if she was just doing it for marriage, it probably would never appease my father. He would always hate you." If she wanted honesty, she was going to get it.

I put my hand on hers. "Can't we relax just a little bit? Why can't we just have a fun evening and see where it goes from there?"

She finally smiled and shook her head. "You guys—all the same..."

When she did drop the marriage topic and settled into normal date conversation, I discovered that all she could talk about was the film industry and her exercise regimen. She was a fitness addict who worked out at least three hours each day.

We went on to Barney's Beanery in West Hollywood, where we played pool and drank pitchers of Bud. Deirdre seemed to know half the guys there. I was beyond any jealous feelings at that point and just concentrated on our game of pool while considering how the evening was going to end.

When we left the bar, she asked me to follow her in my car to make sure that she drove home safely. We parked in front of her apartment, part of a two-family house in the Hollywood Hills, which had a breathtaking view of the city. I was surprised when she invited me in, as I thought she'd want nothing more to do with me. Still, maybe she liked that I hadn't pandered to her. I'd been thoroughly honest with her about my intentions.

We began making out as soon as we stepped in to her dark apartment. Her kiss combined the disparate tastes of Marlboro Lights, Budweiser, and Chanel. Locked in an embrace, we staggered into her bedroom and fell together on the bed. I was pretty blitzed, which was when I was most fluid in my advances. I began my roaming hands routine, but when she abruptly got up, I thought it was "good night" time. Instead she reached over me to the night table, handed me a condom and left the room. I quickly threw off my clothes and got under the covers, waiting contentedly.

"Hi there," she coyly said with a smile as she emerged from the bathroom nude. She shut the lights, climbed into bed, and hugged me, her body warm against me.

"I'm glad you're not angry at me anymore," I whispered.

"I wasn't ever *angry* at you."

After a mechanical and alcohol-shortened session of lovemaking, she turned on her side and began setting her digital alarm clock. I was already an afterthought, as she began planning for tomorrow. I climbed out of bed and searched for my clothing on the floor. While getting dressed, I acutely felt the role reversal.

As I drove home, I engaged in a postdate review and analysis. Our businesslike copulation seemed to demand one, and I laughed aloud at the thought. Unlike other one-night trysts, however, I felt no guilt or shame, unsure exactly who had taken advantage of whom. I would say it was mutual.

So, this was sex in L.A. "NO!" I said aloud. This time, I was not going to overgeneralize. This episode was less representative of L.A. than of social life in the nineties. It was more about two people who craved intimacy in an age of AIDS and marriage anxiety. I could easily have had the same experience in New York or any big city in the United States. It's just that in L.A., the women were much better looking and the drive home a bit longer.

CHAPTER 8

'Tis strange—but true; for truth is always strange;
stranger than fiction.

LORD BYRON

"**A**s a favor to me, Everett, take the assignment," said Harriet of the temp agency. "It's the only assignment we have today, and besides, we're in a recession, you know." That damned recession again—I'll bet she couldn't even define the term. Yet she invoked it every time she wanted me to take a lousy job. Lately I was beginning to feel like Job, tested by the Right Connections women to see if I was committed to this business. In the past few weeks, they had given me temp assignments in places that were only tangentially connected to the film industry. I worked as a secretary at Hollywood Records, Disney's music subsidiary, as an animator's assistant, and as a gofer in a film financing company.

I needed the money, however, and didn't want to disappoint Harriet. The ladies from the Right Connections always made you feel like if you turned them down when they needed you, they would never call again. Still, this new post horrified me: the Engineering and Maintenance Department at Columbia Pictures. I wondered if I would need to wear overalls and hip boots and be forced to clean urinals. From Harriet's description, though, it sounded like this was a desk job, one of those blue-collar jobs in a white-collar guise. Just in case, I made sure not to wear my best clothes.

As I drove on the 405 south, I tried to think positive thoughts. I knew that with this assignment, I had sunk to a new low. Just a year earlier, I had been studying advanced management techniques for Fortune 500 companies. Still, I believed that every humiliating experience brought me one step closer to my lucky break. I wasn't sure anymore, however, where I wanted to end up. I had not admired most of the creative executives I had met thus far, but I wanted to make it big more than ever. I hungered and lusted for a power position in development, sensing my hypocrisy the whole time. I was learning too well the mantra of Hollywood: Fame, power, and money were more important than how you acquired these talismans. Nonetheless, I clung to the belief that my outlook would change dramatically once I became an insider.

I spent twenty minutes frantically running around the bowels of the Columbia studio lot (or was it now Sony?) in Culver City. Of course, no one I asked knew even vaguely where the maintenance offices were. I finally located a tattered, chipped metal sign that read ENGINEERING. This was definitely miles from the chi-chi air-brushed perfection of the production offices. No show-biz clients here.

I stepped into an office that could have been placed in the Smithsonian as an exhibit of 1950s office furniture. I took my place at the secretary's black metallic desk marked with coffee stains and scratches. Judging from the photos taped to her computer, I was replacing a short, middle-aged black woman who liked to party in Mexico, loved her many cats, and had one special guy in her life who looked like Herve Villechaize, Tattoo of *Fantasy Island* fame.

She also had some standard-issue ditties taped to the wall and desk, the pithy sayings about life that secretaries the world over seem to cherish. One in particular, called "If I Had to Live My Life Over Again" kept catching my eye. It was all about riding more merry-go-rounds and picking more daisies.

Bernie Weinstock, the supervisor, ambled over to welcome me. Mustached, wearing glasses, thin as a rail, with salt-and-pepper curly hair, he was the archetypal ex–New Yorker who moved to L.A. twenty-five years ago to escape that "hellhole" and wouldn't dream of returning back east. ("Who needs the aggravation and the freezing cold?") The nicest thing about Bernie was that he was willing to chat with me when he had a free minute. Of course he always had a free minute; they operated here with a different sense of time and urgency than that of other studio departments.

Bernie had gone to City College in New York and majored in history, and through a series of disparate career moves in the film industry had wound up as supervisor of the engineering and maintenance crews on the MGM lot, which was taken over first by Warner Brothers and then by Columbia. He was an ally when I complained about my job search difficulties, and commiserated with me about the studio executives' lack of humanity.

"Honest to God, they're not bad people on their own, but I'm tellin' ya, something happens to these guys once they make it to the executive office..." I leaned back in the chair, eagerly awaiting a good tale.

"I knew one fella who was known as the biggest tyrant at the MGM studio. He went through secretaries like some guys change socks. He yelled and screamed like a maniac and threw things at his assistants. He once threw a huge paperweight at a junior executive— the guy ducked, luckily, and it ripped a hole in the wall about yea big." He held his hands about a foot apart. "I know, being that I corked that sucker up myself. Anyway, one day I go to the guy's house on the weekend to deliver a cabinet—they were always using us maintenance guys to do personal work for them. This guy's wife answers the door. Big woman, as I recall. 'MILTON!' she screams, and—I swear to God—this meek milk-toast of a man walks out and helps me carry the cabinet off the truck. Doesn't say one word—not a peep. I could hardly recognize him. When I tried to help move the cabinet inside the house, the woman gives me five bucks and says, 'Don't worry, Milton will take care of it from here.'"

Bernie stopped for effect and brushed his mustache down a few times with his fingers. "Now, how do you like that? Mr. Power at the studio reduced to a total wimp by his wife at home. The guy could never look me in the eye from that day on."

Bernie's stories were like black-and-white photos from the forties and fifties of smiling movie stars arm in arm with studio executives. His tales seemed to hark back to the grand and simpler times of Hollywood. I got the feeling that he longed for those days when, even though the executives were still bastards, at least the rank and file interacted with them. These days, it seemed, the crew in Engineering rarely got a glimpse of the top brass. Now they were only dealing with snotty twenty-two-year-old assistants. The only evidence of the executives visible to them was the expensive imports in the parking lot.

My job was interesting in a weird way. I was working in the office to which all complaints got routed. Broken locks, faulty air-conditioners, squeaky doors, cockroach sightings, power outages—you name it, these guys had to deal with it. I had made these calls when I worked in the studios, and now the tables were turned. I'd roll my eyes heavenward when the assistants would condescendingly and painstakingly explain the most routine task.

"Hello, Maintenance? This is Jeanie in Amy Pascal's office. Listen very carefully. The toilet in the women's bathroom on the second floor of the Thalberg building is stuffed up. In other words, the toilet is overflowing with water and can't be used. Send a plumber to come with a plunger and unclog it. It's the last stall on the right, the one with the overflowing toilet and an OUT OF ORDER sign on the door. Tell them to come right away. Did you get all that?" No one, it seemed, had any faith that the people in this department had any brain matter at all, or that the workmen could be counted on to fix the problem in under a month.

I got a kick out of the workmen who meandered through the office during the day. These guys lived out the Marlboro Man fantasy: mustached, wearing cowboy hats and boots, chain-smoking Marlboro Lights. They sported humongous belt buckles and pinkie rings inlaid with jade. These were men who clearly lusted for the seventies, as there was no paucity of polyester in evidence. No Lean Cuisine for these guys either; they proudly swaggered with their considerable bellies hanging over their belts. And Cancun, Mexico, was at the end of their vacation rainbow, as far as I could tell.

Then there was the chief of the whole enterprise, Liam McCarthy. This white-haired Irishman had been around the studio since the late forties. Studio administrations had come and gone, but this man who controlled the guts of the studio lot had survived them all, like the Russian apparatchik who outlived several Soviet dictators by knowing the system and how to circumvent it. He had a ruddy complexion and a cheerful demeanor.

I had a clear view into his office, and *what* an office. On one side was the largest photo of John Kennedy I have ever seen—at least five feet high. The office was also decorated with golfing knickknacks and green-colored Irish memorabilia imprinted with sayings: IRRESISTIBLY IRISH; PATRICK WAS A SAINT—I AIN'T; GOD CREATED WHISKEY TO KEEP THE IRISH FROM RULING THE EARTH.

"I've been to Dublin twice," I said as he passed my desk one day, hoping to draw him into conversation.

He smiled and cocked his head at me. "Ya have now, have ya? That's wonderful! Ya know, Haim Herzog, the president of Israel, is from Dublin," he said in the heavy brogue of his youth. "Sure, *large* Jewish community in Ireland with beautiful synagogues. Very well-to-do businessmen too, don't ya know. Actually, they say the Irish are the missin' Hebrew tribe." You could tell he'd used the same line on all the Jewish studio executives. I felt like I was in a Woody Allen film, confronted by a Christian who viewed me as if I were clad as a Hassidic Jew.

I spent a pleasant week in that office. But as I drove home after my last day there, I couldn't help but feel frustration. What did it say about this industry when the nicest guys I had met were in the maintenance department?

Aside from strange temp jobs, I was also going on some peculiar job interviews. Most were in response to help-wanted ads in *Variety* and the *Hollywood Reporter,* buried in the back of the papers amidst the real estate ads for Malibu beach houses. I rarely recalled the ads when I was called for the interviews, but that wasn't surprising. I sent an average of one letter a day in response to these ads. I knew it was positively futile, as these were usually lousy jobs, and even if they were worthwhile, each ad attracted hundreds of resumés. But at this point, I couldn't afford not to respond.

It was during this desperate period that I encountered Murray Krupnick. He called and told me he was responding to my letter and resumé, which I had apparently sent in response to his ad for an assistant in the *Hollywood Reporter.* Krupnick explained that he was a former songwriter who was now producing and developing TV game shows and needed to replace his personal assistant. I don't know why I consented to a meeting—it wasn't even close to what I wanted. However, I was in a vulnerable mood and would have interviewed for a movie usher position at that point.

I navigated my Corolla into the semicircular driveway of a swank high-rise apartment building on Sunset Boulevard. "Two blocks from Spago's," Krupnick told me proudly. The Mexican valet gave me the once-over, said something in Spanish to his partner, who started laughing hysterically, and slowly sauntered to my side of the car. He could smell power, and I reeked of powerlessness. "Eh, how long you think you're gonna be?" he asked, no doubt to gauge just how far he could bury my car from sight. The Rolls-Royces and Porsches, I noticed, flanked the front curb lest their owners accidentally touch pavement with their Ferragamo soles. The opulent marbled lobby and the oak-paneled concierge desk reminded me of my grandfather's apartment building in Manhattan. Heavy perfume and muzak wafted through the halls. A real swinger's pad, perfect for the nouveau riche.

I stood in front of number 706 and hesitated, debating whether to turn around and run, then took a deep breath and rang the bell. The door flew open, and Krupnick greeted me, holding a cordless phone in one hand and a glass of white wine in the other. "Hi, one sec," he mouthed in an exaggerated way and pointed me toward a garish purple velvet couch as he continued his phone conversation with a steady stream of "uh-huhs." A tiny white poodle materialized (we used to call them punts, because you always had a perverse desire to kick them like a football) and began barking furiously. He snapped his fingers twice, and the dog retreated. As I walked through the foyer I was astonished, for the walls were layered with rows of framed gold and platinum records. All were awarded to Murray Krupnick, songwriter extraordinaire of the disco era. The last time I had heard any of the songs by the singers and groups he had written for was at my 1977 bar mitzvah party.

I sat on the couch and stared at thousands of self-reflections from the mirrors that covered the walls of the living room. I smiled a few times, watching myself watch myself from every possible angle. The effect was dizzying, and I wondered whether it was vanity or lack of taste that had led Krupnick to decorate his apartment in this fashion.

I turned my attention to my host. His face was very familiar to me; it fairly screamed "Jewish middle-aged man from Long Island." He wore his thinning hair with one side grown long and flopped across to cover the recess between. (I always wanted to ask these middle-age guys who they thought they were fooling.) He was wearing a navy velour Fila warm-up suit with the jacket zipped halfway to expose a gold chain with a "Chai" pendant. Good lord, did this guy know the seventies were two decades behind us? He put down the phone, sat across from me with his legs crossed, and stared at me. I cleared my throat as I grew nervous about his intentions.

"First of all, do you go by Everett, or Ev, or what?"

"Everett's fine."

"Okay, Everett it is. You're probably wondering what it is I do. As you saw from those gold records out front, I wrote many of the songs which my good friends made famous. Now you're a little young, twenty-six or twenty-seven I'd guess, but you still probably recognize most of them." He rattled off the names of a dozen sickening staples of lite FM play-lists.

"Wow," I exclaimed. "You wrote those? Those are great!" Well, maybe I was exaggerating a tad, but I couldn't believe that all those songs of glamor and love were written by such a nerdy-looking guy.

"Yeah, I did. But, I no longer 'write the songs.'" He made the sign for quotations with his fingers. "Nowadays, I have two main pursuits. Firstly, I develop game shows." He waved his hands at me as if to cut me off. "I know, I know what you're thinking—tacky and schlocky. But I was surprised to learn that there happens to be big money to be made in game shows. Just take a look at Mark Goodson, Bill Todman, Merv Griffin...*big* money. But you watch these shows and most are such *dreck*, you know? So I figured I could do no worse. Anyway, to make a long story short, I'm on contract to develop a few along the same lines as *Tic Tac Dough* or *Win, Lose, or Draw.*" While he talked, he kept fidgeting and shifting positions in the armchair; the only other person I'd seen with these mannerisms was the brother of one of my father's friends who was an ex-con and always high on drugs.

The poodle padded alongside him, and he picked it up and slowly petted its head while staring intently into my eyes. "So tell me, Everett, you're from New York too?"

"Yup, all my life except for the last couple of years. I was born and raised in Brooklyn and lived in Manhattan for six years, mainly on the West Side."

"I just *love* going back east to the City," he said, standing up and sitting down in midsentence. "Do you know the Russian Tea Room?"

"Yeah, on 57th Street, next to Carnegie Hall." The address was about all I knew, other than that it was frequented by show-biz types, very expensive, and probably twenty years beyond its prime.

"I always go there for lunch with my mother when I'm in the City. They have such wonderful perogi and blini with caviar." He paused, a dreamy expression on his face. "Excuse me for a sec." He abruptly left the room and headed to the kitchen. I expected him to return with drinks for us. Instead he came out several minutes later red-eyed and sniffling, unable to hold my glance for more than a second. "I got this terrible cold," he said. Sure, and I have a Porsche parked outside. "So, Mr. Krupnick—"

"Please, Murray. Mr. Krupnick was my father."

"Okay, Murray. What is this second project? You mentioned you're working on two separate things."

He looked puzzled.

"You know...You said game shows were the first project and that you're doing something else too?"

Seconds of silence passed before the synapses in his brain fired. "Oh, right, right...What was I thinking? Thanks for reminding me. Sometimes I don't know where my mind is. The other thing is the Krupnick Agency Inc. That's the talent agency I've recently formed. I'm trying to fill in the gaps which places like CAA or ICM can't or won't fill. Basically, the idea is that I'm going to handle performers who were once famous but have since fallen on *tzuris*—that's Jewish for hard times."

I smiled. "I know—I'm from Brooklyn."

He laughed. "Right. That's funny! Anyway, I can relate to these people through my own experiences, and just try to help them resurrect their careers. My target is actors like Mark Hamill, J. J. Walker, Cheryl Ladd—I'm sure you and I could come up with a bunch more."

I smiled as I spoke to soften the criticism. "I'm just playing devil's advocate, but don't they have representation already? And no offense, but what can you do for them that they haven't already tried?"

He sighed and stared at me. "I can empathize, Everett. Empathy is one of the greatest emotions known to man. You and I both know that those sharks who are called agents in Beverly Hills couldn't care less about the artists. They just want to make a quick buck off them. And when things get rough, do you think they stick by you? You're history, yesterday's news, leftovers. I know from personal experience where these people have been." He put his hands on his heart and looked like he was about to cry. "I have been there and know how they feel. That is 90 percent of what they need."

"Interesting," I said, nodding my head vigorously. "But what does the assistant position entail?" I had at least to find this out before I left.

His face brightened. "Right, the position, or as the French say, *la position*. My administrative assistant of many, many years recently left, and so I need someone who's going to work very closely with me. My assistant, or you if you're chosen, will come to work here in my apartment, help me with mail, correspondence, phone calls, and organizing my life. Second of all, the assistant will help develop the game shows. We'll be writing sample game show questions together, side by side, which will require research skills. And thirdly, you'd be helping me get the Krupnick Agency off the ground."

"Hmmm...Sounds like a lot to do...Interesting..." I was just filling in the pauses with meaningless comments, trying to find an appropriate moment to leave.

"You're probably wondering what it pays, right? They always ask." He seemed to be talking to the dog. "The answer is, a decent amount to start and plenty more if we succeed. I'll start you at $18,750 because you have good experience, and we'll see how it goes from there."

"Umm-hmm...umm-hmm...umm-hmm." I was speechless.

"So, do you think you'd be interested in this sort of thing? I admit I was surprised to get your resumé but it was too good not to call you."

"W-well, I'm close to deciding on a few other jobs. But your position does sound interesting, though." I paused, as if contemplating the choice. "Well, listen...umm...why don't we do this: I'll think it over and you think it over, and if we both think it's a good fit, we'll talk further." How was that for Hollywood-speak?

"Great. Just let me know within the next few days, because I have a lot of other really terrific candidates to call." He reached behind him and grabbed a huge stack of letters, testament to the desperation of the wannabes.

I leaned over to stand up.

He waved me down. "Wait, wait—before I forget, I want you to try something." He walked into the dining room and brought back several plastic bottles, which he set out in front of me on the coffee table. He held one out to me, and I could see it was moisturizer.

I looked up at him puzzled. "Go ahead, try some." He scooped up the dog and petted it as he watched me squeeze some lotion on my fingers and rub it on the back of my hands.

"Nice," I said, smelling my hand. "What is it?"

"The whole line is amazing—the shampoo, conditioner, shaving cream. All natural, all hypo-allergenic. Have you heard of Nu Skin?"

I frowned and nodded slowly. Nu Skin was a skin care and nutrition products company based in Utah, which distributed its products through a pyramid-style direct sales organization like Amway. You joined the company as a salesman by buying a $35 starter kit. Theoretically, you could make money by selling the products, but you soon learned that a more effective way was to enlist others to become salespeople by selling them kits. You could then sit back and share in the commissions earned by them, as well as by any other salespeople they enlisted, and so on.

"I know what you're thinking, and I was skeptical too. But a woman whom I love very much has turned me on to Nu Skin, not just for the quality of the products, but how much money I see her making. If you—"

"Listen, Murray, I'm sorry, but I *really* have to run," I said, standing up. I couldn't deal with this guy anymore.

"Here," he said, handing me a folder and putting his hand on my shoulder. "Take these materials and let me know what you think. Even if you don't work as my assistant, maybe you'll be intrigued by the unlimited potential of Nu Skin."

I thanked him, grabbed the folder, and headed out of the apartment. Once in the hallway, I ran to the elevator banks and jabbed at the DOWN button. I leaned my head against the wall and emitted a quiet scream of anguish for wasting my time humiliating myself. Not just a ridiculous job offer, but a Nu Skin sales pitch on top of that. My father was right—once you leave the beaten path, it can get weird and ugly out there.

CHAPTER 9

Fellow MBA

*Over in Hollywood they almost made a great
picture, but they caught it in time.*

WILSON MIZNER

"**Y**ou've been very patient these
past few weeks, very patient," Harriet said. "I know the assignments
haven't been the best. We do think you're ready again now to take on
some of the more high-profile assignments." Thank God. I was being
released from the temping purgatory that had begun after the
Kirkpatrick debacle.

I was excited when she told me that my assignment that week
was to temp for Robert Cort, head of production for Interscope Films,
an independent production company. *The* Robert Cort who had
produced many successful, albeit formulaic, movies for Disney like
Outrageous Fortune, Cocktail, and *Three Men and a Baby.* I knew
his background quite well, as I had researched it before writing him a
letter—which had promptly been ignored. His career intrigued me
because he had come from the business world and yet had become so

successful on the creative side. I studied his progression, hoping to get some clues about making such a transition.

Cort had graduated magna cum laude in history from the University of Pennsylvania, was a Wharton MBA, had worked for the CIA in the early seventies, and had been a management consultant with McKinsey. He had gotten his start in the industry as a consultant to Columbia Pictures, examining their sales and distribution system. He was then hired by Columbia, and later Fox, in advertising, publicity, and promotion. Somehow, he segued into production at Fox as executive vice president, where he oversaw production of *Romancing the Stone, Cocoon,* and *Bachelor Party,* among others. He then partnered with Marshall Field department store heir Ted Field to found Interscope (Field's worth was estimated by *Forbes* at over $700 million). He was also half of one of Hollywood's inbred power couples: His wife was Rosalie Swedlin, who was then a prominent agent at Creative Artists Agency (she eventually left the agency to become an independent producer).

"And this is the telephone and that's the typewriter," Pam, the overly friendly blond receptionist at Interscope, explained to me, mouthing each word slowly and looking at me intently to see if I comprehended. I nodded studiously. Had there been a camera focused on me, I would have turned to the audience with a raised eyebrow.

My patron whizzed by me at ten-thirty, grabbing his call list from the desk as he walked by. Well, so much for a heart-to-heart conversation with a fellow Ivy Leaguer. As he shouted on the phone behind a closed door, I voyeuristically flipped through his power appointment book. I concentrated on the all-important lunch and dinner schedule, which determined one's rank in the Hollywood pecking order. His schedule of meetings with agents, executives, and movie stars certainly qualified him for a position on the Power 100, the annual ranking published by *Premiere* magazine, over which the industry obsessed.

Each time Cort walked in and out of his office during the day, I looked for any opening to converse with him. I kept rehearsing the talk I'd have with him, how I'd casually mention that I was a fellow MBA. Of course, he'd feel obliged to invite me into his office, and we'd chat like old friends. When I did muster the courage to tell him that I too had gone to business school, he muttered something like "That's great" as he walked into his office. I felt pretty stupid. We did converse later when he asked me to do some simple phone and typing tasks, but he was in no mood to chat with a temp, and we never did have that heart-to-heart talk.

The next day he left his door open, and I could at least eavesdrop to pass the hours. He was whining to a colleague:

"I'm so tired of this shit—you have no idea. I know I'm being obsessive-compulsive, but that French fucker is driving me crazy. Francis says to me yesterday, 'Bob, you can't take away my vision for zees project.' *Vision*—vision with a fuckin' tits-and-ass scene in a teeny-bopper film. I says to Francis, 'I'm gonna jump from the fourteenth-floor window and someone else will take my place and tell you the same goddam thing.' I mean, at the end of the day, it's my ass on the line, right? This whole project is becoming a nightmare for me."

I knew the project that he was talking about. Interscope was in the midst of filming *Welcome to Buzzsaw,* a comedy about the travails of a yuppie investment banker starring Matthew Broderick and directed by Francis Veber, one of France's most successful comedy writers and film directors. It was unusual in that it had been written by twin brothers, Joshua and Daniel Goldman, who had also penned *Darkman.* I had snagged a copy of the script and read it the night before. It was so poorly written and full of plot holes and clichés that I was depressed after reading it. It disheartened me that a script I *knew* was horrendous was being made by a major production company and was able to attract a sizable budget.

The film cost $21 million and was eventually released two years later by Universal Pictures as *Out on a Limb* (no relation to the book by, and made-for-television movie starring, Shirley MacLaine). Even *Daily Variety,* whose reviews almost always found something positive to say, called it "a moronic comedy that leads the pack as the worst film of the year so far." The entire plot hinged on a piece of paper in the yuppie's wallet on which was written a phone number that was supposedly worth $140 million.

The blurb from the film's video box referred to it as an "outrageous comedy." The only outrageous aspect was that this film was made at all. When I finally viewed it on video, I was amazed by the final product. With all the creative executives involved on the project from Universal and Interscope, how could they have released such an unmitigated disaster? Were Cort and every other executive connected to the film aware, I wondered, that they were on board what would become a horrible car wreck? And how in God's name did they manage to spend $21 million with only one A-list actor in the budget?

I felt vindicated. I didn't know if I could tell which script would become a blockbuster, but I did feel confident judging when a script was a total mess and should not be developed further.

Later that day, I peered again into Cort's office, and he was now lying splayed out on a black leather couch. He began what I now recognized to be his end-of-call mantra: "Ah-huh, ah-huh. O-kay, all right. Ah-huh. Ah-huh. O-kay. Mmmm. O-kay." With each response he slowed the pronunciation, placing more emphasis on each word. "Mmmm-hmmmm...Uhhhh-huhhhhh...Alllll riiiight...Greaaaat ...Gotta run—let's do lunch sometime. Love ya...Ciao."

I did everything I could to pass the time in his office productively. I read all the memos and scripts the company was involved with. I retyped his Rolodex cards. I tidied up all his files and folders. I called everyone I could think of. After a while, though, all I had left to do was shift the Scotch-tape dispenser and stapler around on the desk. Still, I enjoyed the time spent in his office. Though he said very few words to me all week, he also placed few demands on me and was far from abusive.

One afternoon I devoted to delving through a six-inch stack of resumés and cover letters, a pastime I found fascinating and cathartic. Flipping through them, I got a clear overview of my peers. From all over the country and with all sorts of degrees and experience. Successful people in law firms, advertising agencies, and investment banks, with fancy titles and salaries. All absolutely convinced that moviemaking was their ultimate destiny in life and sure that Cort was the man who would make it happen. And yes, to my horror, I found my own, once crisp, letter and resumé tucked inside. I smiled at how naive I had once been, expecting a cold letter to generate any significant response.

I also read some fantastic cover letters, which made me realize how anemic mine had been. One imaginative letter from a U.S.C. film school graduate spent the first five paragraphs interconnecting the applicant's fall from a bicycle as a child to his years as a free-style skier to his stint as a "high flier" on Wall Street, culminating with his desire "to fly again" with a major production company, such as Interscope. So here was this great letter by a film school graduate, and it too was in the middle of the reject pile.

One day, Cort handed me a letter that had arrived by Federal Express. It was from a recent New York University film school graduate who was going to be in L.A. for a week the next month and wanted to herald his arrival and arrange a meeting with Cort. What *chutzpah* to FedEx it! Were gimmicks like this what it took, I wondered? Nope. Cort relegated the letter to the resumé pasture with a concise "File this."

I longed to call some of these people and tell them what I'd learned: "Hi, Steve, this is Everett. You don't know me, but please believe me—you have a better chance of winning Lotto than getting a worthwhile job in Hollywood through a cold letter." I'd further advise them that they'd be better off staying in Illinois or Florida and maintaining the fantasy and illusion that they harbored about the movie industry. Still, I knew well the strength of their passions and that the only way to fulfill their dreams or root them out was to come to L.A.

During my week at Cort's office, humorous events occasionally broke the monotony of temping. One day, a gaggle of smiling, bowing Japanese men in three-piece brown and navy business suits appeared, ushered through the office by Pam. As the flavor of the month, Japanese investors were courted aggressively by Hollywood producers. JVC Entertainment had invested $100 million in a joint venture with producer Larry Gordon (*Die Hard, Field of Dreams, Predator*), software developer ASCII Corporation had committed $15 million to producer Edward Pressman (*Wall Street, Talk Radio, Reversal of Fortune*), Carolco Pictures had received $60 million from Pioneer Electronics for a 10 percent stake, and Morgan Creek had gotten $100 million from a division of Nomura Securities. Robert Cort, I noticed from his appointment book, had been to Japan for several days the previous month. Later, I found out that Interscope had formed a film production and marketing joint venture with Disney and Nomura Securities.

Casting calls for upcoming Interscope productions were entertainment in themselves. One day they auditioned women for the role of a prostitute. A parade of slutty-looking women dressed in black garter belts and leather miniskirts passed by me. They lined up in the hallway, each in her own world. Some pulled their hair from one side to the other, while staring intently ahead. Others practiced their lines aloud. ("Damn it, Tony, I'm a human being!") There were "whores" of many varieties: white, black, Asian, lusty and sultry, buxom and petite. I smiled and tried not to drool.

Watching Cort, you'd never guess that he worked amidst such nuttiness. Throughout the week, I noticed his facial expression was one of mild depression. He rarely smiled in front of others; only on the phone did he truly come alive. It seemed as if he related well via electronic communications but had little patience for face-to-face interaction.

Just like Kirkpatrick, this man at the top of his field evidenced little joy. Cort reminded me of the crusty old producer who snapped at his employees, "They don't call it show art—they call it show business!" I knew the film industry was a business, but it wasn't exactly insurance or steel! Somehow, I expected the film executives to personally evince this difference. And once again, all I could do was silently pledge that, given the chance, I would be different. You could count on it.

CHAPTER 10

Spock

*Strip away the phony tinsel of Hollywood and you'll
find the real tinsel underneath.*

OSCAR LEVANT

As a temp, I never knew where I'd
end up working next. Each episode was a fly-on-the-wall opportunity
to briefly enter the life of another Hollywood character. And as I
earned back her trust, Harriet continued to send me out on some of
the choice assignments her agency received. After all, you need to
send your best person when Spock calls.

I laughed after I got the call to go to Leonard Nimoy's production
office. As I got dressed to leave, I tried to think what I knew about
Nimoy. Spock and *Star Trek*. *Star Trek* and Spock. That was about
all I, or most people, knew about the guy. But, like every other
famous or semi-famous actor in Hollywood, he had his own production office and staff. Nimoy's company was called Rumbleseat
Productions. Actors often give their companies these cutesy names,
like All Girl Productions (Bette Midler), Itsbinsolong, Inc. (Shelley

Long), Jabberwacky Productions (Ted Danson), and Siren Films (Madonna). Other than some well-known exceptions (like Michael Douglas, Robert Redford, Clint Eastwood, or Jody Foster), I had heard that the majority of these production offices were a joke. The actor did one or two projects per year, yet the staff was forced to sift through hundreds of scripts just to make sure that they were not turning down the role of a lifetime. Plus, they ended up spending much of their time handling personal errands for the star. These offices were known as "housekeeping" or "vanity" deals, whereby studios subsidized stars, directors, and writers by allowing them to develop their own material. In return, studios received a "first look" at these projects.

Studios viewed these deals as the cost of locking up the talent for future movies. The studio might have to make a lousy film once in a while, but it was worth it to have a relationship with a top star. For example, Paramount had made *Razor's Edge* for Bill Murray in order to get him to star in *Ghostbusters,* and had made *Days of Thunder* (dubbed *Top Car*) for Tom Cruise after his success in *Top Gun.* Studios recouped the housekeeping costs (overhead alone can easily reach $500,000) by charging them against the ensuing films' budgets. This raised the films' costs, making it all the more difficult for them to break even. Paramount had convincingly demonstrated this in the *Coming to America* trial in which Art Buchwald had tried in vain to locate the film's profits.

I wandered to the back of the Disney lot and reported to a wooden trailer named Zorro #4 (this being Disney), which was subdivided into various production offices. The interior of Rumbleseat Productions consisted of a secretary's desk and waiting area, Nimoy's spacious office to the left, and his development executive's office to the right. The secretary's desk area was a jumble of *Star Trek* memorabilia: busts of Spock, crocheted rugs of Spock, photos and pictures of Spock, Spock coffee mugs and dishes, pencil erasers shaped like Spock. What a joke!

I sat behind the secretary's desk and began nosing around. After reading some of the memos lying on the desk, I opened the minifridge to check on the beverages. I popped open a Diet Coke—not because I was particularly thirsty, but because it was 9:45 in the morning and I was sensing a long, boring day. I drummed my fingers on the desk while thinking of people to call.

I decided to check in with Alix Madigan, a blond midwesterner and a recent Wharton MBA who had gained admittance to the creative side of the business. She worked in development at an independent film company, Avenue Pictures. I had met her for lunch several weeks earlier and got a kick out of talking to her. She was a neophyte in Hollywood with a WASPy upbringing and was particularly enamored with Yiddishisms.

"Hey, Alix, how's it going? It's Everett Weinberger."

"Oh hi, Everett. Wait a sec—"

Music wafted in my ears. *"...you shared my dreams, my joys, my pain, you made my—"*

"Bubby, you know I—No, John, it's the other set of notes. Hang on."

"...and now that we've come to the end of our rainbow—"

"I'm telling you it is so busy here. I have to schlep all this—No, John, not that one. Stay with me."

"...you're once, twice, three times a lady." I was beginning to get annoyed.

"Bubby, I'd like to kibbutz more—"

"You'd like to what?"

"Kibbutz, you know, chat." Right, now the WASP was trying to teach *me* Yiddish words.

"I know what it means. It's just that the word is *kibitz,* not *kibbutz. Kibbutz* is a cooperative farm in Israel. I just thought I ought to point that out to you."

"Whatever..." She wasn't pleased to receive a linguistic lesson at this moment. "Listen, things are a little crazy here. Plus, the air conditioner is on the blintz." Now that was a new one—remaking an

English phrase into a Yiddish one. I let it go.

"I've gotta run, but you're okay, right?"

"Sure...Great...Never been better."

As I put the phone down, I heard loud singing, the kind that's usually confined to the shower.

"La dee, da da da, la dee, da da da. DEE, DEE, DEE. La, la, la. Dee, dee, da, dee, dee."

A short woman suddenly appeared in the doorway, dressed in a bright multi-colored silk shirt and a black miniskirt, and smiling expansively with an elfish gleam in her eyes.

"Hiya, you must be Everett. I'm Rita Crespo, Leonard's assistant." She was a rarity in Hollywood among executive assistants, being well into her forties (though from afar, with her short brown hair and dangling earrings, she could have passed for the same age as the other assistants). She was also obviously a free spirit, and I immediately liked her. I did wonder, however, if she was slightly nuts or just eccentric.

I jumped to my feet and muttered something about letting her sit behind the desk.

"Don't worry about it, honey. You get used to the whole setup. I'm just here in the morning to show you the ropes—not that this is rocket science, you know." She flopped down in the armchair in front of the desk and casually pulled her panty hose up. This woman had no inhibitions.

She saw me staring in wonderment and thought I was thinking something else. "Yeah, this is a crazy business, huh? But you've got the bug up your ass, like all of them. What's your story? What do you want to be?"

"Well, I'm temping now while trying to land a production executive job at one of the studios."

"Oh, one of the hot shots, huh? You want to be a top gun? Are you one of those MBAs from back east who got tired of investment banking?"

I stared at her, dumbfounded, and laughed. "Not bad!"

She chuckled. "Too close for comfort, huh? Well, at least you're young and hungry. That counts for a lot in this business. I've been with Leonard going on, let's see...five years now, and I'm finally ready to leave so I can work in physical production for a studio. Physical production's what I do for Leonard when we have a film shooting. We relocate our office to the on-site location. During our last film for Paramount, *Funny About Love,* I functioned more like a production coordinator. And I gotta tell you, I loved it."

"So why don't you just go for it *now,* Rita? No one is forcing you to stay."

"Why don't I? Honey, you don't know the Catch-22 of these assistant jobs. You do an excellent job, which I've done for Leonard day in and day out, and they don't ever want to let you go. Leonard knows he'll never find someone as good as I am or who knows him as well. So if it were up to him, he'd keep me here forever. But I can't just up and leave, since I need his help if I want to move on. All he has to do is make one or two phone calls and I can work anywhere."

"He's really that big a deal?" I snickered. "I thought all he's done his whole life is play Spock." I guess I should also have told her that I hated *Star Trek* and could not understand the whole Trekkie craze. I had always fought with my older brother whenever he changed the channel to watch the *Enterprise* boldly going somewhere.

Rita looked at me with a combination of amazement and anger.

"Ev, Ev, Ev! You have no clue at all. No clue. None! First of all, he's also a proven director—he directed *Three Men and a Baby, The Good Mother, Funny About Love,* and two of the *Star Trek* movies. Second of all, he's not just an actor, he's an icon, an industry. Every *Star Trek* film he's been on, the entire studio brass at Paramount has personally met with him and begged him to do it."

"You mean he doesn't like to be Spock?"

"Like it? He loathes it. He wants to move on with his life."

"Well, it's his choice, isn't it? I mean, he's done five *Star Trek* movies, and he's probably made tens of millions on them." (Nimoy would soon do a sixth one in 1991, although he bowed out from the seventh installment in 1994.)

"Sure, but after twenty-five years it's a ball and chain around his neck. Think about it. He can never escape it. He even called his autobiography *I Am Not Spock*. Please, he is *not* just a faded actor. He is a god to people out there all over the world. He gets recognized and mobbed wherever he goes—even in Japan or Europe or Australia."

She grabbed a file from the desk. "Here, let me show you what I mean. Look at this." She handed me a manually typed, smudged, four-page letter from some guy in Montana who had also written poetry to Spock about some obscure *Star Trek* elements.

I laughed as I read the letter. "Now I know what William Shatner meant when he was on *Saturday Night Live* doing a skit of a *Star Trek* convention and he says to the Trekkies, 'Get a life!'"

Rita didn't smile. It was all too familiar to her. "You have no idea, none." She showed me photographs Trekkies had sent Nimoy of themselves with their families and pets in their backyards.

"People think of him as their close relative."

"How pathetic."

"Damn straight. And this is just a couple of days' worth."

I absentmindedly played with some small colored stones that lay in a porcelain dish on her desk. They were smooth and polished, and I liked their feel.

"Those are my New Age stones. Somehow, they help relax me. You like 'em too, huh? I knew I had a good feeling about you."

I smiled at her, while continuing to play with the rocks. "Hey, Rita, tell me something. I looked in at Nimoy's office—it seems way too clean and tidy. Doesn't he ever come in to work here?"

"Sometimes, but lately not much. He works from home with his wife Susan or from the set when he's shooting. So you probably won't be seeing much of him, although he'll call in for messages." She grinned at me while peeling a hard boiled egg, the first of many items she ate with zest.

Rita stayed with me throughout the morning, entertaining me with tales of the industry. She was taking the rest of the week off to get a face-lift. It was the only way she felt she could compete against the influx of perennially young development girls in the business.

As far as I could tell, the office got approximately ten phone calls a day. The director of development, Bill Blum, stayed in his office and answered his own calls. I assumed that since the studio paid the overhead for these offices, the production companies always preferred a live body sitting in the office to an answering machine. I made a mental note to bring in plenty of reading material for the week ahead. I could knock off a *Vanity Fair, New Yorker,* and *Premiere,* just in the morning.

The only other activity in our trailer came from the office across from us. I was curious about it, since all I saw was a guy and a woman, both in their early twenties, clad in shorts and T-shirts. I learned from Rita that this was the production office shared by J. J. Abrams and Jill Mazursky. Fresh out of college, they were working on rewrites of *Taking Care of Business,* a screenplay about a yuppie who loses his Filofax, which they had sold for a ludicrous sum and which eventually resulted in a horribly unfunny comedy starring Jim Belushi and Charles Grodin. Both writers had huge career jumpstarts, Mazursky from being the daughter of director Paul Mazursky, and Abrams from hooking up with Mazursky.

The only time I had contact with Nimoy was when he called in for his messages. "Good morning," the former half-Vulcan said in his slow, deep baritone. "This is Leonard Nimoy checking in for messages." His voice was so familiar that I was tempted to yell, "Hey, Spock, how's it going?" It must have been annoying and disconcerting for these stars when they appeared in public and strangers greeted them as if they were old friends. It was no wonder that many of them, like Nimoy, had become reclusive.

At lunchtime, I locked the office and strolled along the deserted and spotless alleys of the lot toward the Disney commissary. As I passed by, I peered into various carpentry shops or scenery storage warehouses, ever curious as to what went on in each of the buildings. "What film is that for?" I'd ask authoritatively, as if I were an executive on a plant tour.

The manicured grounds, as well as the homogeneity and youth of its populace, gave the studio lot a collegiate feel. Just like at school, everyone there seemed to converge at the cafeteria during lunchtime. And akin to the college bookstore was a Disney company store where proud employees or awestruck visitors could purchase Disney-logoed clothing and merchandise.

Unlike at most studios, at Disney even the senior executives ate at the commissary. No time for three-hour lunches here. I grabbed a tray and headed for the salad bar. I kept seeing people I knew from informational meetings or from my round of creative executive interviews. They all nodded at me and quickly turned away when they realized where they knew me from.

I sat down in the outdoor patio near a table of junior creative executives who were eating hamburgers and french fries in near silence. I felt free and relaxed in comparison to this listless, nervous-looking group. Many of my friends in conventional jobs, like Neil, Anton, or Alexandra, seemed to be more spontaneous, energetic, and outgoing than these people. I had heard that Disney hired their creative executives to three-year contracts, which were viewed as prison terms. These people certainly looked as if they were waiting to complete their sentences so they could join other studios or production companies. It was not for nothing that Disney's nickname in the industry was "Mausechwitz." It's a special kind of studio whose working conditions are compared with those of a concentration camp.

I came home Friday night after my week in Spock's office to find a handwritten note in my mailbox from Anton. He loved the romance of good stationery and a mysteriously worded note written in his flowing script.

Ev,

Be ready for an adventure tomorrow morning at 9:00. Bring bathing suit, sunglasses, and the right attitude.

Salut,
Anton

The next morning, I came downstairs to meet Anton and found him smoking a cigarette near the mailboxes in the lobby. He wore a navy beret, tilted on his head at a jaunty angle. I could have predicted the rest of his outfit: penny loafers without socks, faded jeans jacket, plaid Bermuda shorts, Persol sunglasses.

"Do you realize what a Eurostereotype you're becoming?" I said, laughing. "All you need is a blue-and-white striped shirt, a bicycle, and a baguette sticking out of your knapsack."

He laughed and took off the beret. "Actually, this was just for your amusement." He slipped on a Yankees cap, and as we headed out the front door, grabbed my shoulder. "You're in for a treat—I decided to bring Kristie. She's absolutely amazing."

"Please, tell me she has a twin sister and you've brought her along for me." I took Anton's word on his women very seriously, as I had seen several of his previous conquests. Though he was by no means ugly, his looks were unconventional. Yet he attracted and dated some breathtakingly beautiful women. His poise and confidence counted for much.

"Sorry, no twin. But if you're good, I'll let you do her," he said with an evil Jack Nicholson grin. "And believe me, that is no small treat." He always had to let me know, preferably in an off-handed way, when he had scored with a woman. It gave him added pleasure to share the secret.

I bowed to the inevitable and followed him out to the circular driveway, scanning the cars for his unmistakable Cadillac. Instead, he got into the driver's seat of a white Cabriolet convertible. Sitting alongside him was a woman whose beauty made me want to bang my head on the nearest wall and cry, "Ow, ow, ow!" She had the flawless looks of an air-brushed magazine cover photo.

I hopped into the back and leaned over the two front seats as Anton maneuvered the car onto Wilshire Boulevard. I felt like a dog left in the back seat with its tongue lolling in excitement. Anton looked at me through the rearview mirror, and I mouthed, "Wow."

It was one of those clear, warm, perfect L.A. days that made you feel that weather alone was reason enough for living in the city. Kristie turned around to greet me, her blond hair flying in a slow-motion arc across her cheeks, like some B-movie close-up. Her face was inches from mine, and she stared at me with her emerald eyes. "You must be Kristie," I managed to say. "I'm Everett. I've heard a lot about you from Anton."

"I hope all good," she said, and leaned over and playfully sucked Anton's earlobe, which caused him to swerve sharply. He put his hand on her naked thigh and squeezed.

"Hey, what about me?" I whined and pouted in an exaggerated manner. I dreaded being the third wheel for the rest of the day.

She laughed and pushed me back into the seat. "Maybe later."

I bounced back eagerly, my eyes drawn to her midriff-baring T-shirt. "Anton tells me you work at Elektra Records—that's really cool. What area are you in?"

"I'm in A&R." A&R, or Artists and Repertoire, was the department in record companies responsible for discovering and developing musical talent (akin to the studios' creative executives). A&R executives hung out in clubs, signed up new bands, and then guided them through the recording process. For music lovers, it was a dream job.

Anton had told me that Kristie used to date a guitarist from the hard-rock group Metallica, who got her the job. Coincidentally, or perhaps as a shrewd business move, she dropped him soon after she began at Elektra.

Anton turned on the radio, nearly blasting me out of the car. Aerosmith's "Janie's Got a Gun" blared as we cruised westward along the Santa Monica Freeway.

I leaned over and lowered the volume, which Anton promptly raised again. "So, Kristie," I yelled, "what's your musical taste like? Do you like groups like Aerosmith?"

"Oh, I *love* Aerosmith. They're great. They're making a huge comeback."

Minutes later, Eric Clapton's "Layla" came on. Kristie pealed with joy. "Oh, I *love* Clapton." I rolled my eyes at Anton in the rearview mirror; he caught my glance and grinned.

Kristie *loved* everybody the deejay played. When the Clash's "London Calling" came on, I couldn't resist a quick reality check. "Now *this* is music," I said. My Stanford housemate, Mitch, was a Clash fanatic and had constantly played their albums. "Do you like the Clash, Kristie?"

"Of course. I *love* them."

"Really? Me too. What's your favorite album?"

"Uh...I like the one they released a couple of years ago."

"Gosh, Kristie, I could have sworn the Clash broke up in 1983."

"Umm, well, you know, I-I mean their greatest hits album they released a little while ago."

Anton began giggling. She punched him in the arm. "Anton, tell your friend he's being mean to me."

"Be nice, dude," Anton said sternly.

"I'm sorry, Kristie, I didn't mean to talk shop." Yes I did. I knew I was being an idiot. But I was tired of getting coffee for marginally literate entertainment executives, and here was one I wasn't working for. The target was just too tempting.

I soon learned that we were headed to the J. Paul Getty Museum in Malibu via the Pacific Coast Highway. I had always wanted to visit the billionaire's museum, built in 1974 to house his enormous art collection. It was a painstaking reconstruction of the Villa dei Papiri, a Roman seaside villa buried in volcanic mud when Mount Vesuvius erupted in the first century, destroying Pompeii and Herculaneum. With the largest endowment in the museum world (over $3.5 billion, or nearly eight times larger than that of the Metropolitan Museum of Art), the Getty Museum had undertaken an aggressive acquisition program to augment its collection of Greek and Roman antiquities and Impressionist paintings.

"Hey, Anton—what about the parking restriction? I've heard that reservations are usually booked weeks in advance." Since museum parking was limited, visitors needed reservations for the parking lot.

"Trust me, I have a plan," he said dramatically, and leaned over and kissed Kristie on the lips, while going over eighty-five miles per hour in the passing lane.

Anton shared my love of a good loophole to bypass annoying rules. He had found a clever way to get around the Getty's requirement. We parked on a side street a few blocks from the museum, waited at a bus stop for the number 434 city bus, took it one stop, and got off with a special museum entrance pass in hand. The museum allowed people to arrive via mass transit, a dispensation to the lower-income residents without cars. Of course, museum officials and city planners could do little to stop people like Anton from exploiting this chink in the armor.

Anton, like most Los Angeles residents, railed constantly about the traffic and smog, yet would sooner move out of L.A. than give up his car. In a *Los Angeles Times* poll, 40 percent of the respondents said they believed that cars had ruined the city, but over 80 percent had not been on a city bus in over a year.

We walked through the museum exhibit halls together. Kristie displayed an uncanny ability to flirt with both Anton and me simultaneously. She was expert at the brush of a hand, the squeeze of an arm, the touch of her hair on your face. She might not be much of a music historian, but was adept at linking us together as a threesome, and I was grateful.

We ended up outside in the back garden, with its beautiful imported mosaics and geometrically planted flowers and shrubs. "Hey, guys, look at that mos—" I paused in midsentence, as I turned around to see Anton and Kristie making out in front of a Greek statue. They looked great together, but then again, Lurch from *The Addams Family* would have looked good with Kristie.

Afterwards, we stopped for a quick lunch at Carlos and Pepe's, a Mexican restaurant on Pacific Coast Highway that served lethal margaritas. At the height of the midday sun, we stumbled out and drove north to nearby Zuma Beach, having changed into bathing suits in the restaurant bathroom. We draped our towels on the sand, and Kristie took off her T-shirt to reveal a fluorescent pink bikini, which showcased her even tan and gym-toned body. Anton and I knelt on the warm towels and prepared to lie back, stare at Kristie, and let the alcohol slowly dissipate from our systems.

"Oh no you don't," Kristie said, as she grabbed the two of us by the hands and pulled us to our feet. She linked arms with ours and we ran together into the cold surf, splashing and laughing. Anton hugged her tightly and kissed her, as I dutifully pretended to be absorbed in body-surfing. Later, the three of us leaned back on the wet sand near the shore as the waves gently cascaded over us. Kristie, in the middle, put her arms around Anton and me, her cold, smooth skin reminding me why celibacy and Los Angeles were not compatible.

Style meant everything to Kristie, and all her actions were geared toward looking good from any angle. Each of us had implicitly been assigned a role for the day in this MTV video, directed by Kristie. Anton played the part of the lucky guy who has a beautiful girlfriend and magnanimously shares her company with his friend. Kristie, of course, was the perfect leading lady, laughing her way through the day and engaging in spontaneous mischief. I was assigned the role of the good-natured but single friend of the couple, who allows them their private moments but joins in the group fun.

"What a perfect day," I said contentedly as we lay in the sun, having had my best day in L.A.

But as we climbed into the car and the sun began its descent, our J. Crew fantasy came to an abrupt end. Now, with my wet bathing suit, and the sand in my crotch dribbling onto the seat and floor of the car, I realized that I was going back to the everyday life of flossing my teeth, waking up with hangovers, and catching colds. Anton and Kristie, however, shared a fierce desire to create perfect moments and limit the frequency of the distasteful and mundane.

I had to admit that those fleeting moments had more intensity than a thousand ordinary days. I had come to L.A. and continued to stay because I believed that this fantasy life was attainable. I'd watched many of my friends "settle," on schools, jobs, wives, lives. You have to compromise at some point, they reasoned. But I didn't want to. Not yet, at least. That was something I could do later, in my mid-thirties, when all else failed. Until then, I would cling to the desperate hope that everything would fall into place: career, wife, happiness, even self-actualization. My life might then mirror the illusions advertised so prominently in film, television, and fashion catalogs, or proselytized in countless infomercials by personal success guru Tony Robbins. I knew I shared those feelings with Anton, Kristie, and the Hollywood crowd.

"Reality ends here" was the unofficial motto of USC's School of Cinema and Television, but could easily have been the theme for the city. This was the proposition to which the city of Los Angeles and the movie industry were dedicated. Like the proverbial chicken and egg, it was hard to say whether the movie industry created the L.A. image or vice versa. True, the city did have some natural competitive advantages over most places with its sun, beaches, and palm trees. But it was the Jewish studio founders from Europe who galvanized this philosophy and embodied it in their films when they created mythologized versions of America.

The longer I stayed in L.A., the more I too was drawn into this web of fantasy. I couldn't claim immunity from the seductive tentacles of the Hollywood lifestyle. The power cars on the freeways, polished to a mirror finish, so clearly out of reach but always there to remind. The showcase women, who seemed to me like another commodity in L.A., an inevitable accessory of the power elite. The mansions in Beverly Hills, which I passed every day on my commute to work, attended to at all hours by hordes of Mexican workers.

I'd be lying to say I didn't want any part of this life. And yet, I squirmed when I acknowledged this blatant materialism; I knew it was not the answer. My hunger for having it all had not abated, however, even while I criticized every aspect of the system, including the players within it. I kept asking myself: How can I continue lambasting these people while lusting for their jobs and lifestyles? This was a textbook case of cognitive dissonance, and I knew that I could not live with my hypocrisy for much longer.

CHAPTER 11

The Middlemen

You can take all the sincerity in Hollywood, place it in the navel of a fruit fly, and still have enough room for three caraway seeds and a producer's heart.

FRED ALLEN

I anticipated my next temp assignment with eagerness. A chance to work inside Creative Artists Agency, ground zero and home to Hollywood's (and according to its denizens, Planet Earth's) most powerful citizen: chairman Michael S. Ovitz. Not to mention that this was the talent agency of over seven hundred of the industry's top actors, directors, and screenwriters. If it was a big name, chances were excellent it was on CAA's client list. Nearly every top-grossing film since 1984 had been staffed with CAA talent.

Ovitz and four other renegade agents from the William Morris Agency had founded CAA in 1975, and by the mid-eighties it had become the most powerful agency in Hollywood through the packaging of films, a technique Ovitz had learned from his years as a television agent. CAA took scripts written by its screenwriter clients, attached as many of their actor and director clients as possible to the project, and then sold the whole deal to the studios as a package. These film packages maximized CAA's cash flow, raised stars' salaries to new heights, and gave the agency enormous clout with its clients and with the studios. For instance, *Rain Man*, the Oscar winner for Best Picture in 1989, was packaged by CAA and featured actors Dustin Hoffman and Tom Cruise, producer Mark Johnson, and director Barry Levinson, all CAA clients.

I arrived at their $16 million I. M. Pei–designed temple on the corner of Wilshire and Little Santa Monica Boulevards after leaving my car with a valet in the underground garage (imagine, valet parking even for the temps). This place gave new meaning to the word "slick." From the humongous twenty-six-foot Roy Lichtenstein mural in the cavernous lobby to the trade magazines arranged at sharp right angles in the waiting area (I imagined a diagram dictated by Ovitz that specified the exact placement of the magazines), CAA was on the cutting edge of cool.

As I sat on the leather sofa near a gargantuan ficus tree and waited to be brought to my desk, I watched this beehive of activity. Three sleek, beautiful women at the front desk curtly greeted visitors while answering the steady flow of calls. With their sharply pulled-back hair and their lightweight headsets, they looked like extras from a cyberspace film. Young trainees in white shirts and ties bustled on the second and third floors, which faced open to the atrium. There was something Zen-like to this well-orchestrated scene; Ovitz was, after all, a devotee of Far Eastern thought and philosophy (each morning he practiced aikido, a Japanese martial art form in which he was reportedly trained by CAA client Steven Seagal). It was often reported in the press that each summer, like the Japanese, he planned his life out in three- and five-year segments.

I was assigned to Marcia Spano, an MBA in her early thirties who had worked on the business end at Columbia Pictures for Victor Kaufman, then president and CEO, and in commercial banking prior to that. What was such a financially oriented person doing at a talent agency? I discovered that the rumors were true—Ovitz had created an investment banking boutique within CAA to work on Hollywood mergers and acquisitions deals. I listened dumbfounded as Marcia explained that Ovitz had hired Sandy Climan, a thirty-four-year-old Harvard MBA, to run a corporate finance department within the agency.

Ovitz was now in the business of brokering entertainment conglomerates. He was no dummy; he saw the astronomical fees Wall Street mergers and acquisitions departments were garnering, which made his talent agency fees look like chump change (perhaps he secretly envied his Birmingham High classmate, Michael Milken). Ovitz played a major role in negotiating Sony's $3.4 billion purchase of Columbia Pictures Entertainment in 1988 (for which CAA received a $10 million fee), and during my mini-stint at CAA he was advising Matsushita Electric Industrial Company in its effort to acquire MCA (Matsushita landed MCA later that year for $6.6 billion).

Ovitz further extended CAA's domain into the realm of corporate consulting and advisory. CAA was retained in 1991 by Coca-Cola as a worldwide marketing and communications consultant. Using CAA writers and directors, the agency produced television commercials for Coca-Cola, a revolutionary departure from Coke's forty-year advertising relationship with McCann-Erickson. CAA also teamed up, in 1993, with Nike to promote and market sporting events worldwide.

That same year, CAA was retained by Crédit Lyonnais, a French bank, to help it manage its troubled $3 billion media and entertainment loan portfolio, and to help find strategic investments in those industries. The bank's portfolio was littered with bad loans to such companies as Cannon Pictures and Carolco Pictures, but its most pressing problem was Metro-Goldwyn-Mayer, the fabled studio it took over in 1992, which it had to sell by May 1997 in order to comply with U.S. banking laws. Crédit Lyonnais had initially lent funds in 1990 to Italian financier Giancarlo Parretti of Pathé Communications for his purchase of the studio from investor Kirk Kerkorian. When Parretti failed to turn MGM around, the bank ousted him and assumed control of the studio. The Crédit Lyonnais assignment was the classic CAA situation: a desperate outsider to Hollywood with lots of cash who craved the connections and prestige of Ovitz & Co. Ovitz, in turn, was able to use the studio as an employment agency of sorts for his clients. This was made easier when he installed Frank Mancuso as chairman and ex–CAA agent Mike Marcus as MGM president. (Rival Jeffrey Berg, chairman of ICM, asked the Justice Department's Antitrust Division to investigate CAA's relationship with Crédit Lyonnais.)

By 1995, Ovitz was busy flying in cyberspace. He was negotiating with Bill Gates, chairman of Microsoft, on a joint venture to produce interactive television commercials and programs. He also hired Robert Kavner, president of AT&T's Multimedia Products and Services division, to head CAA's new media group. They soon announced a joint venture with three of the regional Bell telephone companies to create a video-programming network for telephone customers on the East and West coasts.

Though the finance skills from my investment banking days could have been put to good use, I was not allowed to do much for Spano while working there. The activities of this office were too confidential for an outsider to view. As a struggling temp, I would have been sorely tempted to utilize the inside information. (The Matsushita/MCA deal, which they were then working on, would eventually and ironically result in the implication of the president of MCA's son, Jonathan Sheinberg, for insider trading.) Throughout the day, packages arrived for Marcia from Simpson, Thatcher & Bartlett, a Wall Street law firm involved in the Matsushita negotiations. The area felt more like Goldman Sachs than a talent agency.

I was impressed that all the CAA employees had Macintosh computers—and not PCs—at their desks, linked together on a network. In 1990, it said a lot about the progressiveness of a company when it abandoned the standard IBM format for the Macintosh. I was also surprised by the security controls placed on the system. Initially, the computer was open for use, and I began browsing through files containing script coverage, client assignments, and contract terms. I felt like Woodward and Bernstein reading secret Pentagon files. I gulped as I read, knowing that this information was priceless to most of the creative executives in Hollywood. After running an errand, however, I came back to find that the computer was shut down. When I turned it on again, I couldn't open up a single folder or program without typing in a password. The place was like the CIA (and only one initial apart). I felt guilty, though I knew there was an implicit expectation in Hollywood that information was fluid and eventually known by all.

Spano was extremely friendly to me, once she learned that I was a fellow MBA. I honestly didn't know, however, why they had called for a temp, as she did not ask me to do much and there was voice mail on the phones. I felt like an operator who pushed the buttons inside an automatic elevator.

The CAA stint rekindled my desire to learn more about agents in order to decide whether I could ever envision becoming one. I lost count of the number of times I was advised to become an agent. Nearly every executive I met with had told me of all the famous ex-agents who were running Hollywood: David Geffen, Barry Diller, Mike Medavoy, David Hoberman. The skills you learned and the contacts you made as an agent were supposed to match exactly what was needed as a production executive.

It was also possible to become an agent without a traditional film background, which was why many viewed agency mailrooms as the closest thing to Hollywood training programs. But in order to become an agent at a major agency, you had to begin in the mailroom. Lawyers and MBAs pushed mail carts in various agencies for $250 a week for a year or longer, waiting to "get on a desk" and become an agent's assistant. A sane person might ask why working as a messenger, delivering flowers and gifts, moving file cabinets, and picking up dry cleaning was the perfect training for an agent. The answer: location, location, location. In those jobs you were well positioned to become part of the whole process of getting noticed by the agents, competing with your peers, reading every letter and script you could get your hands on, and uncovering useful gossip about Hollywood power brokers. I heard at least three versions of the story about the enterprising trainee who was immediately promoted for fixing an agent's broken chair while the agent was at lunch.

Still, I had my doubts as to whether I had the temperament necessary to be an agent. In terms of professional respect, agents seemed to be held in the same light as lawyers, bookies, or drug dealers. One joke making the rounds at the time:

Question: If you had a gun with only two bullets in it, and were suddenly confronted by Sadaam Hussein, Adolf Hitler, and a Hollywood agent, what would you do?

Answer: Shoot the Hollywood agent twice.

I asked Harriet for the next available temp assignment in an agent's office. She soon found me a one-week stint with an agent named Nick Stevens at a small but influential agency, Harris & Goldberg (which would later become part of Innovative Artists). When I walked tentatively into the agency's offices in Century City the next morning, all heads turned to inspect me. The room of young, hungry agents-in-training was already buzzing with activity at seven-thirty. The sounds of typing and phone conversations, the smells of coffee, danish, and Liquid Paper, assaulted my senses. One young guy in a white shirt and loud tie who looked like he graduated from college an hour before escorted me to my cubicle.

I stared at the phone in front of me. It looked like a lunar module control panel from a cheesy science fiction film. The Brad Dorman-esque assistant bent over and looked me in the eyes.

"Okay, listen very carefully. I don't have time to explain more than once, and you won't have time to ask questions once things get cooking." He grabbed the receiver and pushed a few buttons, and the phone rang. "If the phone rings like this, it's an internal call." He pushed some other buttons, and the phone rang again with a slightly different tone. "If it rings like this, it's external. Put the caller on hold and press star-two and let Nick know who's on. If he wants the call, he'll tell you and you pass it through by pressing CONF and the line. If he doesn't want it, take a message." He paused to exhale. "Now I assume you know the call books."

Thank God I learned something from the Kirkpatrick experience. "Oh yeah, Kirkpatrick at Paramount uses them."

He looked up at me in awe. "You worked for Kirkpatrick? You must know my friend, Brad Dorman."

"Yeah, I definitely do."

"Good guy, huh?"

I resisted the urge. "Yup, he's great all right."

"I'll tell him I ran into you." The assistant continued, but slower and in a friendlier tone. "Okay, back to the phones, which should be a piece of cake for you." Newfound respect. "Now, if Nick's on the phone and another call comes in, press star-five and it will beep in his ear, letting him know he has another call. If he picks you up, let him know who's on. If he then flicks his hand, pass the call through. If he waves at you, it means he wants a piece of paper with the caller's name. If he ignores you, wait a minute and then beep him again." I knew I was never going to remember all of this. "Never, never, never pass a call through without getting a signal." He paused. "That's the easiest way I know to get fired. You're not exactly the first temp Nick has ever had. Okay, I gotta head back to the battlefield. If you have any questions, ask, but quickly. And don't hesitate—Nick hates that."

I muttered thanks and looked again with dismay at the phone. I sat at the desk and practiced pressing the buttons, because I knew it would soon get chaotic.

"Hello gents, hello gents. Top of the morn, top of the morn." A short, tan, wiry guy in a baggy beige Italian suit I had last seen draped on a mannequin at Fred Segal's zipped by and headed into the glass-walled office in front of my cubicle. Methodically, he draped his sport jacket on his chair, took off his John Lennon sunglasses, placed his black Filofax on the desk, and put on a phone headset. He was my age but looked to be about eighteen. His confidence, however, was ageless.

"That's Nick," my mentor whispered from the next desk. Nick looked straight at me and motioned with his hands. "And that's the famous hand signal...Good luck."

I walked in and stood in the doorway. This cocky little guy was my boss. I mustered up a smile, shook his hand, and introduced myself.

He nodded several times as he inspected me. "Nice suit, nice shoes, nice tie." He fingered my tie and turned it over to check the label.

"You approve?" I asked.

He grinned. "I most definitely approve." He quickly turned serious. "Okay, Ev. First thing is speed. You gotta move like you're on fire. Second, always, always watch me so you'll know what I want and when. And, most of all, I need confidence. I need to know I can count on you, Ev. I *gotta* count on you...Can I count on you? I can count on you, Ev, can't I?"

I stifled a smile. "Yeah, no problem, Nick. Don't worry, you can count on me."

He seemed relieved. "Great, great. In just a few minutes I'll be ready to lock and load." Lots of war imagery in this office.

I turned to leave. "By the way, Ev," Nick said, "you do drive and own a car, don't you?"

"Yeah, of course. Why do you ask?"

"Just checking, buddy. Just checking." He smiled (sneakily, or was that just my imagination?) and smacked me on the shoulder. I've never met anyone worth trusting who used the word "buddy."

I headed back to my desk, shaking my head, and leaned over to my neighbor. "Psst! Why did Nick ask me if I have a car?"

"He just wants to know if you can do dispatch. Last temp they sent didn't drive."

I nodded, then leaned over again. "Hey, what's dispatch?"

"Every one of us takes turns driving around for the agents, delivering packages and running errands for them."

As I digested that tidbit, Nick called me on the intercom to let me know we were about to begin. And seconds later, he began his phone marathon.

I've met many schmoozers in my life, but Nick was one of the best I'd seen. I felt like a college basketball player who gets drafted into the NBA and realizes he's totally out of his league. Nick was in constant motion, always talking. His trick was not to let conversations reach a lull. He never had to think about what next to say. He was like a guerrilla—attack and run. Thus, he always left his caller on a high and busy note. With a "Gotta run," he was on to the next call. He would have made a great Wall Street stockbroker or trader. Like trading, it was all confidence, energy, and adrenaline.

Nick was a talent agent as opposed to a literary agent; he represented a stable of character actors: mostly young, up-and-coming talent or over-the-hill performers. I recognized some of them from their headshot photographs. His biggest-name client at the time was Ruben Blades. I figured the big agencies took most of the top stars and the smaller ones were left primarily with the B and C actors.

It was clear why Nick hustled the phones with such vengeance— he needed to make deals for his clients, and hence 10 percent for the agency. And it took tens of B and C actor roles to equal the commission that a Tom Cruise garnered for his agent. Nick was a salesman, pure and simple, just like those at Merrill Lynch, only instead of stocks or bonds, he was selling the services of his actor-clients.

First thing every morning, he reviewed "the breakdowns," a daily publication that lists which film and television projects are casting and provides a brief description of the roles. After he decided which of his clients were appropriate for the parts, he had me pull the actors' photographs and resumés from their files and send them by messenger to the casting offices, usually before noon.

Throughout the day, Nick took multiple calls from the actors, which was part of the constant hand-holding he had to do for his clients. He functioned as a quasi-therapist for some, reassuring them or coaxing them into taking a part. One actor needed an advance to pay the rent, one actress needed advice on whether to get a nose job, another actor was too hung over to make an audition. Nick expertly handled their personal problems with the ease of a professional baseball player taking batting practice.

Nick was also an adept negotiator with the studios. "Our demands are simple," he'd say while standing and counting with his fingers. "First, a trailer equal in size and quality to the other top actors'. Second, a car and driver for morning pickups and night drop-offs. Third, two thousand dollars per week for expenses plus a cellular phone. Finally, she gets her own makeup, hair person, and personal trainer paid for by the studio. Those are what we need to be happy—capisce?"

It was said that you wouldn't want a priest as your agent. Watching Nick maneuver as he negotiated for his clients, I realized why. A "turn the other cheek," gentlemanly approach might impress your parents but would not win your clients the highest pay packages.

When he wasn't on the phone, Nick would often pace in his office with his miniature tape recorder in hand. "Letter to Patrick Mackey address in Rolodex dear Patrick comma thank you for sending us your photos and resumé period we appreciate—no, scratch that—your experience is certainly extensive period however comma I unfortunately do not feel that your background matches the type of clients which our agency represents period let us know—scratch that—I wish you all the best in your endeavors and encourage you to stay in touch period sincerely comma Nicholas Stevens cc: Jodi Levine end of letter blind carbon copy to Susan Cohen and to file."

I was puzzled when he dropped several of these tiny tapes on my desk. As usual, he smelled my hesitance. "You do know how to transcribe, Ev, don't you?"

I nodded dumbly, though I had never used a Dictaphone. It was quite simple, though. And fun: You could slow down or speed up the tape, which allowed me to hear Nick speak as if on amphetamines or Quaaludes.

Once, he dictated a letter to his dentist. I wasn't sure whether to laugh or cry while wearing earphones and hunched in front of a typewriter, listening to him discuss root canal work.

I had never worked with anyone who used a phone headset, and it took some getting used to. Nick would prance around his office while talking out loud, often looking straight at me. In the beginning, I'd mouth, "What," and point to myself, never sure when he was talking to me. I felt like a complete incompetent that first day.

Through a blizzard of phone calls, Nick had an amazing ability to sense exactly when I was unsure about what I was doing with the phone system. He'd immediately seize on my wavering and shout at me.

"What's going on, Ev? HELLO? HELLO? What are you doing? What are you doin' to me? WHAT? WHAT? WHAT?" Everyone in the office would ignore these scenes, but would furtively give me looks of sympathy. They distanced themselves from me as if they expected me to be fired the first or second day and thought it might be contagious.

I did master the phones after two days, and the other assistants were friendlier to me, often exchanging stories with me on work experiences in Hollywood. They also joked about Nick's penchant for firing temps on their first day.

"Whoa, what is that, Everett...four days!"

"Congratulations, Mr. Longevity!"

Nick appreciated my competence and began to treat me with more respect. At the end of each day, he walked me to the parking lot and tried to sell me on becoming an agent. "It's not for everyone, Ev," he said, "but if you're like me and love negotiating and you live for action, there's nothing like it in the world."

Looking at him with his cellular phone, Italian clothes, and flashy car, I did feel seduced by his lifestyle. He didn't realize, however, that the very experience of working for him and watching him in action had made the thought of becoming an agent all the more remote. I didn't think I could ever become a clone of Nick because I wasn't one-tenth as skilled as he was in schmoozing and making demands. And yet, I knew that he was the prototype of a successful agent. Last time I heard, Nick was a rising star and head of the talent department at United Talent Agency, brokering eye-popping deals for client Jim Carrey.

CHAPTER 12

The Producer

Right now, it's only a notion. But I think I can get money to make it into a concept and then later turn it into an idea.

BEVERLY HILLS PARTY TALK IN *ANNIE HALL*

Over six months into my search. I couldn't help but think of my business school classmates all over the country who were advancing in their careers and lives. I was reminded of this by Neil, who was visiting L.A. on business and updated me over dinner. Some had already changed jobs or received promotions. Others were in the midst of starting their own companies.

I concentrated on the small victories in my career as a temp. I was heartened, for instance, to learn that my next assignment would provide me with a fly-on-the-wall view of a quintessential Hollywood producer. After all, producing was ostensibly my ultimate career goal. I was assigned to work for Laurence Mark, who had an independent production deal at Disney. He was the producer of some moderately successful films, such as *Working Girl* and *Black Widow*, knew everyone in the business, and spoke with most of his fellow power brokers each week. His six Rolodexes overstuffed with cards lined his assistant's desk.

Laurence Mark Productions was located in an ultra-modern suite in the Animation Building with a sumptuous office for Mark, smaller ones for his vice president of production and director of development, and two assistant's desks in between. The place was decorated with posters from his films, as well as framed photos of stars like Debra Winger. Across the hall was Martin Short's production office. (I looked inside his office as I passed by and was surprised to see him sitting studiously at his desk. I half expected him to be pacing the room in his Ed Grimley character and chanting, "I couldn't be more excited, I must say.")

Mark's assistant, David, was preparing to go on his yearly vacation to Hawaii. I appreciated David's candor when he discussed what lay ahead for me during the coming week. "Larry can be an animal sometimes," he whispered, "a real animal. He'll yell and bitch and scream and maybe throw things, but don't get flustered. That's just the way he is—he can't help himself. Just keep your cool, go about your business, ignore him, and you'll be fine. He gets angry, but he always recovers and quickly forgets about it."

He spent several hours describing the neuroses Mark had about the running of his office. Ten minutes were devoted to explaining in painstaking detail the placement of the trade papers, the *New York Times,* and the "Calendar" section from the *Los Angeles Times,* which Mark liked to have placed in a stack on the lower right-hand corner of his credenza each morning. Apparently, if you put one newspaper out of order, he would freak out. I also had to learn the mixture Mark liked in his coffee machine: a blend of two types of coffee plus a dash of cinnamon. And I had to memorize yet another call list routine and phone system (by now, I could have become a phone systems salesman). On Mark's Amtel system, his assistant typed the caller's name on a keyboard; when he saw the LED readout at his terminal, Mark pushed a button to communicate what he wanted done with the call. I thought David was being overly punctilious, but the lessons proved invaluable throughout the week.

Monday morning, I was alone in the office for several hours, wondering if this was going to be one of those bogus temp assignments, when a guy my age walked in and asked me to make copies of a script. He conveyed a look of street smarts and channeled ambition—that "stick with me and you'll go places" type of confidence that was so important in this city. He introduced himself as John Baldecchi, Mark's vice president of production. He was surprisingly talkative and inquisitive as to my background. I returned volley and probed him for his take on the Hollywood experience, realizing that with several more years in the industry and a lucky break, I could be in his position.

Baldecchi told me that he was part of a network of young executives who shared information on industry players and new projects. They traded information for favors in a constant stream throughout the day, figuring that their allegiances to each other would one day pay dividends. Baldecchi and his friends, who worked at the major studios, production companies, and agencies, regarded each other as the next generation of executives who would rise concurrently and run Hollywood together, just as the baby boomers were doing now.

"We all know we're going to be running every part of this town in about ten years," he said matter-of-factly, "so we might as well help each other out when we can."

In a display of magnanimity, he showed me the spreadsheet he kept on his computer of jobs currently available in Hollywood production offices. I quickly wrote down the contact persons for the positions, like a hungry rat being thrown some meaty scraps, since I was still talking to as many new executive contacts as I could find, as well as applying for all sorts of permanent positions. I realized, though, why an outsider like me could never find the best vacant positions—this information was doled out as favors to those people in the know.

Just after lunch, Mark walked in. There was no doubt as to his identity; he was yet another short, Jewish, balding guy with a mustache and an attitude in Hollywood. With a wave of the hand, he flew by into his office and immediately had me working the phones for him.

Mark schmoozed just as much as the creative executives at the studios (he was a former production executive at Fox and Paramount), but he was much more involved on the film projects he was producing. He was currently producing *Mr. Destiny* with Jim Belushi and *True Colors* with John Cusack and James Spader. Each day, he was messengered a cassette of "the dailies" or "rushes" (because they were rushed to and from the film lab), which contained the scenes shot the day before. After he viewed it, I dispatched the cassette to the co-producers on the project.

He also received pages with additions or changes to the scripts from the films' production offices. It was a nightmare for me, as I had to keep track of the different drafts of the scripts, each one photocopied on a different color paper. Thankfully, there was an industry color standard for the draft revisions: white for the original draft, followed by revisions in blue, pink, green, yellow, and goldenrod. I'd have ten copies of the script spread out in front of me as I gingerly replaced the old pages with the new colored ones.

I grew to respect Mark's expertise in time maximization. He would hang up his phone and leave the office while speaking on a cellular phone. In under five minutes, the office phone would ring and he would have me connect him with a series of calls. Often, he would put me on hold to take call waiting on his car phone. I enjoyed connecting calls for him, as he allowed me to listen in on his conversations.

He once had me patch in Richard Dreyfuss, who was also on a car phone. Mark was trying to convince Dreyfuss not to drop out of *Randall and Juliet,* a film Mark was preparing for production. I got Dreyfuss on the line and connected the two.

"Go ahead, Larry, Richard is on the line," I said, as if the two were old friends of mine.

"Hi, Richard!"

"Larry, about the project, I just need to—" Oops, or as Homer Simpson says, "Dohh!" I had pressed the wrong button and disconnected Dreyfuss. I was left stranded with an irate Mark who was stuck in a traffic jam on some freeway and on the phone now solely with his lowly temp.

"Wh-what the fuck did you do?" he said in a shrill voice. "Hello, hello, hello? What did you do? Richard? Hello?"

I would have laughed at his squeaky, panicked voice had I not been in serious trouble. "I don't know what happened," I said, lying through my teeth. "The line just went dead. Hold on, the other line is ringing—it must be him."

Luckily, Dreyfuss was on the other line.

"I'm really sorry about that, Richard," I said.

"No problem, kiddo," he said, rather generously.

Given my Kirkpatrick experience, I expected to be fired when Mark returned to the office later in the day, but true to David's word, Mark was quick to forgive and forget, and he never mentioned the incident.

Mark was a little dynamo of energy, running in and out of the office throughout the day. When he had a meeting outside the office at an unfamiliar location, he would ring me on the intercom. "2425 West Olympic," he would say. That was the signal for me to pull out the *Thomas Guide,* the indispensable book of maps that covers every square inch of the city. I'd photocopy the appropriate pages and highlight the most direct route. Then, to make it totally idiot-proof, I typed out the directions. Minutes before the appointed meeting time, Mark would run out, sport coat in one hand, his other outstretched for the directions.

He even got his hair cut in his office. His French stylist arrived for the appointment and paced the office waiting for him.

"Where zee fuck ees he?" she hissed. "Ee ees always late."

A half hour later, all was forgiven when he zipped through the door. She joined him in his office, where he had a professional barber chair. She whipped a smock on him and, while cooing at him, began trimming his hair. Even though he was balding, he apparently liked his fringe hair to look the same from week to week. He even had a writer pitch him a movie idea while he got his hair cut. Now *this* was the Hollywood I had pictured!

Not that Mark didn't work hard for his perquisites; he devoted every waking moment to film. Just as retailing executives had to go out and see the company stores, Mark always made time for nightly screenings or premieres. Even the quasi-vacations he took to attend the film festivals were spent, for the most part, in dark theaters. The festivals, to be sure, were not exactly held in places like Detroit, Naples, or Dusseldorf. But the festivals in Cannes, Venice, Berlin, or Telluride were just trade shows through which the film world propagated an image of glamor and fantasy. I was currently arranging Mark's schedule for January's Sundance Film Festival in Park City, Utah.

Soon into the stint, I discovered that lying was an important job skill for a producer's assistant. When I typed a caller's name into the Amtel, Mark frequently punched the standard "I don't want to talk to him now" button. He left it up to me to provide more creative responses: "He's out on location." "He's on an international conference call." Or my favorite, "He's in his car right now, but he's driving through the canyons and can't be reached."

Another truth-stretching exercise was typing the "pass letters." In·a given month, Mark received hundreds of scripts sent to him by agents or writers. Those that arrived unsolicited and without representation were returned unopened. The risk of a lawsuit was too high, given the similarity of many film projects, unintentional or otherwise.

After being read or at least skimmed by his reader, most scripts were returned with a consolatory note. Since we couldn't write the truth ("You call this piece of shit a script?"), I was told to type something along these lines:

Dear Tom,

Thanks so much for letting us have a look at *Judy and Jimbo's Jamboree*. Unfortunately, we have to pass on it. We would, however, welcome any future submissions.

Best regards,
Larry

I felt it would have sounded more sincere if Mark had signed his own name.

Mark's frequent notes asking me to make all sorts of last-minute schedule adjustments exposed me, as his representative, to the ire of his appointments. I came back from lunch one day to see a note on my chair: "Call the Ivy and tell them to change reservation tonight from 6:00 to 8:00."

I called the Ivy. "Hi, this is Everett from Larry Mark's office. He'd like to change his reservation tonight to eight o'clock."

"Where's David?"

"He's on vacation—he'll be back Monday."

"Oh...Well it's already two-thirty now," he said in a condescending tone.

"I know that. Obviously, something came up at the last minute, or I wouldn't be calling this late."

"Well, I'm afraid that we're full at eight. You should have called earlier."

I hadn't expected this. I was going to have to be a dick. "Listen, I know it's late, but I really need a table at eight. You've got to help us out here."

"I don't *have* to do anything—we're full."

I silently counted to five. "I don't understand your point. I really don't. Look, umm—what's your name?" Long pause.

"Glen. But—"

"Listen, Glen," I sniffed. "You have a choice to make here. Now, either you let me speak to your manager, or give us a table at eight. I don't think you want to be the reason why Larry Mark never eats in your restaurant again. Now what's it going to be, Glen?"

He hesitated. "Listen, I am *really* sorry, but—"

I sensed weakness and went in for the kill. "You have a choice to make, Glen...possibly a career decision. I need your answer right now. Which will it be?"

He sighed in exasperation. "All right, all right. Tell your boss he can have the table. Tell him he should also give you a raise."

I laughed. "Thanks a lot. We really appreciate it. And you should get a raise too, Glen." I guess I too had learned a thing or two about schmoozing.

As I sat in a self-congratulatory mood, Gina Way, Mark's script reader, walked out of the adjacent office. She had been coolly aloof to me from the start, and I had categorized her as a mercurial English major with producer aspirations. She gave me a scornful look as she passed. My face reddened as I realized that she had witnessed the tongue-lashing I had just given Glen. She had just the look of contempt on her face that I had held for Brad Dorman.

Gina's look burned long after the moment. I was ashamed at how easily I had shifted into the aggressor role. I had always believed that, given the chance, I would be different. Was this where I was headed? Were these small, quasi-ethical acts signs that I was willing to do anything to be successful in this industry? And if they were, would I even notice what I had become until it was too late to change?

CHAPTER 13

Blacklisted From the Magic Kingdom

It is amazing how complete is the delusion that
beauty is goodness.

LEO TOLSTOY

Harriet called me in the middle of a
fantastic, erotic dream. I had been enjoying it so much that when I
padded to the bathroom and back at three in the morning, I kept my
eyes closed just so I could continue the dream.

"Good morning, Everett! Rise and shine!" Way too loud and
cheerful for seven-thirty A.M. She sounded like Ethel Merman on
speed. Harriet was calling, however, with big news. "Are you ready for
this?" I had heard that line before. "You do know who Mr. Frank Wells
is?"

My heart raced. "The president of Disney? Of course I know who
he is. Don't tell me what I think you're about to!"

I was very excited. Frank Wells was a big *macher* not only in
Hollywood but in corporate America, thanks to the turnaround of
Disney he and Michael Eisner had engineered. In the early 1980s,
Disney had become a relic, satisfied with releasing several bland

family-oriented features and animated films each year. As a result of its mediocre stock performance and its undervalued and under-utilized assets, Disney came under a hostile takeover attack by financier Saul Steinberg with backing from Drexel Burnham Lambert. With the support of Walt Disney's nephew and major shareholder, Roy Disney, and the Bass family of Texas, Eisner and Wells were placed in charge as chairman/CEO and president/CEO, respectively.

Their achievements at Disney were nothing less than historic. Revenues for the company went from $1.5 billion in 1984 to $10.1 billion in 1994. When the team arrived, Disney was in last place among the major studios with just 3 percent of total box office revenues. By 1988, Disney had moved into first place with over 19 percent of industry ticket sales, and in 1994, Disney was again in first place with a 19 percent market share. Their success was not limited to the motion picture group but included a revitalization of the theme parks and the launching of the Disney Channel and a consumer products company. When the two took the reins of the company, its market capitalization was $2 billion; by 1995, Disney had a market capitalization of $28 billion and was one of the stocks comprising the prestigious Dow Jones Industrial Average.

What I didn't tell Harriet was that I knew Wells's son, Kevin, from Stanford. We had a few classes together, never moving beyond the "how's it going" stage. I hadn't forgotten him, of course, when I wrote down my list of contacts, and had spoken to him shortly after moving to Los Angeles. He advised me to send my resumé to his father, which I did; I was convinced that had led to my round of interviews at Disney.

"Well, if you can get to Burbank in forty-five minutes," she continued, "you've got a week's stint as his second assistant. Just see Tracy in his office and do whatever she asks."

"Done deal. You're a goddess, Harriet." I raced to get showered and dressed for the drive north to Disney.

★

Once on the Disney lot, I headed to the Animation Building, site of those disappointing rounds of interviews several months back. I climbed the stairs toward the rarefied air of the executive offices. If the rest of the building seemed squeaky clean, this floor was air-blasted. People there walked briskly with an air of hyper-importance. "I'm on a mission from God," they seemed to be saying.

I walked past Jeffrey Katzenberg, the diminutive head of Disney production, who administered and shaped every Disney release. He was famous in the industry for his workaholic schedule, his hundred phone calls a day, his pit-bull tenaciousness. Like Eisner, he had grown up as a rich kid in Manhattan, and by age fourteen he had begun working on what would become a seven-year stint for New York City Mayor John Lindsay, dropping out of New York University along the way. He eventually left politics for the movie industry, working as assistant to Barry Diller and moving his way up to head of production at Paramount.

Katzenberg was the counterbalance to Eisner, the nudger alongside the innovator. Eisner was known to call him the Golden Retriever for his consistent ability to sniff out new stars and profitable projects. Katzenberg moved with Eisner from Paramount to Disney in 1984. Referred to as "Sparky" in Celia Brady's acerbic column on the industry in *Spy* magazine, he was the embodiment of those Disney qualities many industry insiders hated: the penny-pinching, the need for total control over creative elements, the formularization of the creative development process, and the night-marish work schedules. Legend had it that when he showed up to work in the early morning hours and spotted other cars in the parking lot, he would feel their hoods to see if the other executives had just sneaked in ahead of him. Alec Baldwin was said to have called Katzenberg the eighth dwarf, Greedy.

Sparky Katzenberg was standing next to one of his secretaries' desks. I nodded at him and he nodded back, thinking I was someone important, given that I was headed purposefully toward the big cheeses' offices. Also, I looked pretty good in my business suit and Hollywood tie, like I belonged in the executive suite. He'd soon learn that I was just another peon, so I enjoyed it while I could.

I continued to the end of the hallway, and sucked my breath in as I saw a knockout blonde with a perfectly toned body. I assumed she was one of Frank Wells's two assistants.

"Hi, I'm from Right Connections. I'm Everett Weinberger." I smiled and extended my hand.

She shook it extremely hard and inspected me. "Tracy Taylor." Blunt, efficient, impassive. Hmmm, now where have I seen this type of person before? It hit me soon enough—she was the female version of Brad Dorman.

"Have a seat. I'll have some work for you in a minute."

I sat at the desk parallel to hers and waited, thinking what my opening line would be when I met Wells.

Tracy placed a huge bundle of mail on my desk. "Here, you can begin slitting the mail and stamping the date on it—always on the upper right-hand corner." So much for executive-level tasks. I was intrigued, however, by the prospect of reading Frank Wells's mail.

Several minutes later, Tracy flicked her eyes at me and noticed that I was doing slightly more reading than opening. "You'll have plenty of time to read later. For now, just stick to opening the letters."

There was a palpable sense of movement on the floor and I knew Wells was approaching. It wasn't that you could actually feel his power, but you could hear and see people's reactions as he passed by.

"Morning, Terry, Anne. That is the prettiest dress." I heard girlish laughter from down the hall. You don't become president of Disney without knowing how to flirt.

"Tracy, have you got the Euro-Disney file?" He called out even before he was in sight. This man knew how to maximize his time. Tracy, in turn, knew how to maximize her brownie points. She had the file stretched out in her hands before he even reached her desk.

"Morning, Frank. That is a great tie."

She pointed to me without taking her eyes off Wells. "Frank, this is Everett Weinberger replacing Sue for the week." I smiled and looked at him expectantly.

Wells grunted and barely turned his eyes in my direction. As he turned to go into his office, and with my heartbeat accelerating, I called out. "Mr. Wells?"

He and Tracy turned their heads toward me in surprise. Tracy immediately frowned and looked nervous. You don't speak until spoken to.

"I know your son Kevin from Stanford..."

He immediately smiled broadly, strode to my desk, and shook my hand.

"Hi! Welcome to Disney. So, you were in undergrad or business school with Kevin?"

"Business school. And I saw you speak on campus last spring." He had visited Stanford and given a speech in Bishop Auditorium on the Disney turnaround story.

He nodded and grinned. "Great, great. Good to have you here!" Touché, Tracy!

After he left, Tracy sullenly gave me some more mindless tasks to do. I realized that my encounter with Wells was strike one in her eyes.

My initial reaction would prove accurate. Tracy was like the hundreds of Brad Dormans who filled the junior ranks of Hollywood. But unlike him, she was a very pretty woman and a skilled flirt, at least with higher-ups she needed something from. The tone of her voice gave away whether she was addressing someone in a position of power or giving a minion an order.

Though Wells did not usher me in as a confidante and give me top-level strategic planning assignments, he did occasionally come directly to me and ask me to run some errands for him. This bugged Tracy, who, understandably, wanted me as far from her boss as possible.

Later that same day, when Tracy was away from her desk, Wells asked me to deliver a package across the lot. "No hurry on that, Everett—just make sure it gets there by two o'clock." I decided to wait and deliver it during my lunch break. Tracy returned, saw the package on my desk, and stood in front of me.

"Did Frank give you that to deliver?"

"Yes. He said to do it when I had a chance, so I'm going to deliver it at lunchtime in twenty minutes."

"I think you should go now and get it out of the way."

"Well, I think it makes sense to combine it with lunch at noon."

"You better go now. Believe me, I know when Frank says 'sometime during the day,' he means *now*."

"But Tracy, he would have said 'Now.' He said just to get it there by two. It's all the way across the lot and—"

"That's twice you snapped at me," she hissed, her face inches from mine. "Don't you *ever* contradict me again because you'll be out of here in ten seconds otherwise. I place one phone call to personnel and you're gone! So *don't* do that ever again! I won't stand for it! Do you understand?"

I stared at her. "I'm sorry, Tracy...I-I didn't mean anything by it." I caved in totally. I was shaking slightly, I was so angry. But if I displayed any of this rage, I'd be fired. Though she was wrong, I had to acquiesce. I managed a really pitiful look and hated myself for it.

"That's all right. Now after you deliver that, you can take lunch early." And with that, she actually smiled. Her transformation was frightening. One minute she was practically firing me; the next, she was my best friend.

Every day, Tracy would leave work with two canvas bags filled with piles of papers and breathlessly, but contentedly, complain to all who were within earshot. "Uhhh...I have so much work to do tonight...so much! Frank needs all of this by nine tomorrow morning." I never could figure out how mundane secretarial tasks could fill two bags with work every night. Wells, after all, had an executive assistant who worked on the more analytical projects. But Tracy was a dedicated Disney staffer, eager to follow company norms.

★

I was on a high later in the week after Michael Eisner said hello to me. Michael Eisner! The cherubic smiling face atop this large-framed body seemed so familiar to me, from seeing him numerous times in print and on television. The forty-eight-year-old executive was the second most powerful man in Hollywood according to *Premiere* magazine (after Michael Ovitz, who seemed to have a lock on the number one position). Eisner had made over $40 million in 1988. (In 1992, he made this sum look trivial when he cashed in stock options worth $198 million.) He was constantly running in and out of Wells's office, which was diagonally across from his own. I admired Eisner, from what I had read about him. I had found and read his "epistle" on moviemaking, which he had submitted to Paramount's board of directors in 1982 and which later became the blueprint for the Disney management style. The centerpiece of the philosophy, in his words, was as follows:

> The pursuit of making money is the only reason to make movies. We have no obligation to make history. We have no obligation to make art. We have no obligation to make a statement. Our obligation is to make money, and to make money, it may be important to make history. To make money, it may be important to make art, or some significant statement. To make money, it may be important to win the Academy Award, for it might mean another ten million dollars at the box office. Our only objective may be to make money, but in order to make money, we must always make entertaining movies. And if we make entertaining movies, at times we will make history, art, a statement, or all three. We may even win awards.

Katzenberg later rehashed Eisner's thoughts in his own twenty-eight-page memo entitled "The World Is Changing," which bemoaned spiraling movie production costs. Sparky's memo was leaked, possibly intentionally, to the press and was faxed throughout the industry, along with a hilarious and insightful parody (which David Kirkpatrick was rumored to have written). For instance, Katzenberg's original: "Disney films mean something very specific. But Touchstone and Hollywood films also reflect a certain entertainment ethic, one that we can be proud of and one that we should continually respect." And the parody: "Disney films mean something very specific. If it's Disney, then it involves some marketable character that we can plaster on everything from toilet paper to disposable diapers. But if a character like Edward in *Pretty Woman* wants to have oral sex with a streetwalker, we must remember to call it a Touchstone or Hollywood film."

Wells, though less known to the public, was no slouch himself in the power department. Whenever I had a free minute, I browsed through Wells's computerized Rolodex. There were power Rolodexes and then there was Frank Wells's. It was a virtual *Who's Who* of both corporate America and of Hollywood's upper tier. However, unlike other mere executives', it did not list anyone below the most senior levels. I guess if you're the king, you only talk to other kings. Let's see, which monarch shall we speak to today: Warren Beatty, Clint Eastwood, Barry Diller, Jane Fonda, Gerald Ford, David Geffen, Bob Hope, Henry Kravis, Henry Kissinger, Michael Ovitz, Robert Redford, Steven Spielberg, or Barbra Streisand? And home numbers too! I called Warren Beatty at home and I swear he answered himself, but I hung up as I couldn't think of anything clever to say. "Hey, Warren, babe! This is your pal and number one fan, Everett Weinberger. I just called to say hi and chit-chat!"

I also skimmed through a book that Wells had co-authored called *Seven Summits*. Piles of them lay behind my desk on the windowsill. The book described how at age fifty, he had quit his position as vice chairman of Warner Brothers, joined multi-millionaire Richard Bass, and, without prior climbing experience, set out to climb the highest mountain peak on each of seven continents. Incredibly, he successfully climbed them all except Everest.

Wells's entire persona was destined to impress. Tall, thin, athletic, bespectacled, with a full head of hair showing silver-gray at the temples, the fifty-eight-year-old Wells looked every bit the role of corporate chieftain. And certainly his education—summa cum laude at Pomona College, Stanford Law School, and Oxford University, where he was a Rhodes Scholar—was more apt for corporate America than for Hollywood.

Glancing at his daily schedule confirmed that it was not merely looks that got him the role. He typically jogged at five-thirty in the morning and had several meetings before he came in to the office at nine. Then the marathon began as countless MBA types scurried in and out of his office throughout the day. Still, the complexity of the Disney empire warranted such vigilance. Disney controlled its multi-division film studios, the cable channel and home video label, the various theme parks in the United States, Japan, and France, and their associated hotels and real estate holdings, a chain of consumer product stores, a publishing venture, a record company start-up, and God knows what else. And here I was, puny temporary employee and creative executive wannabe, sitting at Wells's secretary's desk and expectantly waiting for him to capitalize on my talents. Who was I kidding?

The more I saw of what Wells's position entailed—oversight of all the technical operations typical for a multi-billion-dollar corporation—the more I was sure that he was far more integral to the company than most outsiders knew. Unlike CEO Eisner, Wells apparently had no need to continually seek the spotlight. But Eisner the creative showman and leader was not Eisner the financial whiz. Much of what we had learned in business school about managing a professional enterprise seemed to have been handled by Wells. Finance, strategic planning, real estate, and negotiations all seemed to fall under his rubric.

Wells died tragically less than four years later, in April 1994, in a helicopter crash while he was on a skiing trip in the Ruby Mountains of Nevada with Clint Eastwood. I knew the impact on Disney would be profound, especially after Eisner announced that he would be assuming Wells's duties. Somehow I doubted that either he or Katzenberg, who pined for the number two position, could or would want to do the unglamorous tasks Wells had mastered: negotiating labor contracts, overseeing public debt and equity transactions, or restructuring Euro-Disney.

Wells's death and Eisner's decision would lead like falling dominoes to the tumultuous departure of Katzenberg and his subsequent formation of a new studio with Steven Spielberg and David Geffen (named DreamWorks SKG), and to the destabilization of MCA, which housed Spielberg's Amblin Entertainment and was chafing under Japanese ownership.

There was no way that Eisner, who probably viewed Katzenberg as a younger, less polished version of himself, was going to cede the presidency and its complications to someone so unlike Frank Wells. You don't easily replace a Rhodes scholar with a high school graduate. As one Disney insider said in *Vanity Fair*: "Frank Wells was the highest of high *goyim*. He represented everything Michael wanted to be."

"Congratulations, Everett!" A female voice blared through the phone receiver, waking me up from an unfitful sleep on Friday, my last day at Frank Wells's office. Doesn't anyone sleep past seven in Hollywood? My mind went blank for a minute before I recognized Barbara Dreyfus's throaty voice. It had been six days since my first-round interview with her for the position of assistant to Alec Baldwin.

"You did very well. Let's just say that based on what I told him, Alec loved you—and *that's* an understatement...Heh-low! Are you there? Aaaa-lekk Baldwin wants to meet you!"

"Th-That's g-great," I stammered.

"You bet your (*crackle*) that's great. I'm having (*hiss*) see only three people (*crackle*) my number one choice (*crackle, hiss*) car phone (*crackle*) tunnel (*crackle*) today at five-thirty, okay?"

I thought of the horrors of having to ask Tracy if I could leave work early, and shuddered. "Actually, is Monday possible? I have to work for Frank Wells today at Disney until six." I thought name-dropping would aid my cause, but it had no effect on Barbara.

She seemed slightly miffed. "No, it most definitely isn't. Alec is in town just until tomorrow and is flying to Brazil with Kim for several weeks and then (*hiss, crackle, crackle, hiss*) when he'll be back. Now if you want this *amazing* position which is yours for the taking, I suggest you be there today...All right?" Why doesn't she hype me just a little more about this job?

"Okay, okay. Today will be fine then."

"Terrific. Knock 'em dead, Ev!"

An hour later, I was on my way to Disney. I took the scenic route through Beverly Hills, as I needed extra time to think. I drove along Beverly Drive, one of my favorite streets in the city. It was L.A. as a picture postcard, a dizzying array of multi-million-dollar mansions built behind two perfectly spaced rows of fifty-foot palms that flanked the road. The street seemed to reach its apex at Sunset Boulevard with the otherworldly perfection of the lush, salmon-colored Beverly Hills Hotel, known as the Pink Palace. Built in 1912, the hotel was now owned by the Sultan of Brunei.

As I followed the stream of cars snaking north along Coldwater Canyon toward Burbank, I rehearsed the conversation I had to have with Tracy in my mind, not liking any of its variations. I needed to leave an hour early, and I knew that she was not going to like it.

"Tracy, I've got a very important interview." "Tracy, I'm feeling really sick." "Tracy, my brother is getting married tonight." "Tracy,

I'm going to beat you to death with this stapler if you don't let me go."

I arrived at quarter to nine, a bit late due to the horrendous traffic. She hadn't come in yet. I frowned; clearly, something extraordinary had to have happened for Wonder Girl to show up late for work.

She rushed in at nine-thirty looking uncharacteristically disheveled and immediately got on the phone, sobbing to her friends: She had smacked her gorgeous red Jeep Wrangler into a school bus. She was fine, but the Jeep was a mess. I symphathized with her, but soon grew weary of the story, having heard it at least twenty times, as she told it to everyone who came in or called.

I waited until later in the morning when she had settled down to her work. "Uh, Tracy?"

"Uh-huh?" She didn't look up from her desk.

I opted for honesty. "Tracy, I need to leave an hour early today for a very important final-round interview." Her head jolted up and I spoke faster. "Believe me, I wouldn't ask if it weren't crucial or if I could get out of it. The interview's at five-thirty, so I need to leave here at five. I know today's a bad day for you, but is it okay with you?"

"Sure...sure, no problem. Don't worry about it—I'll be fine." Well, that seemed a tad too easy.

Ten minutes later, Tracy called me on the phone in the file room. "Harriet of Right Connections is on line two for you."

I picked up line two. "Everett, how can you do this to us?" Harriet wailed.

"It's just not professional," chimed in Pauline.

"Wh-what are you talking about?"

"You can't just leave a job in the middle." "It's just not professional." Two on one again.

"You have an obligation to Disney and to us." "It's your last day there, anyway. We know you'll do the right thing and stay."

"Wait a minute..." My hand involuntarily began massaging my suddenly throbbing temple. "First of all, it's just an hour early.

Second of all, I asked Tracy for permission not ten minutes ago and she said okay—no problem."

"Please, Everett, Disney is our most important account and Frank Wells is the president, for God's sake." "Don't do it, Everett, you've gotta stay."

"But she just said it was totally okay! Wells is out of the office on business, anyway. There's not much to do here today. And why didn't she say anything to me?"

"She sure did say something. She immediately called the head of Human Resources at Disney and screamed about the temps at Right Connections." "She just had a very severe car accident, for God's sake. She may need to leave early for the hospital to get an X-ray."

"Hospital?" I sneered. "She looks fine to me. Listen, if it'll make you feel better I'll talk to her right now, and if she asks me to stay, I promise you I'll stay. No problem at all..."

"That's all we're asking." "Do the right thing."

I hung up the phone and walked slowly back into the office and stood in front of her desk.

"Tracy?"

She looked up at me with an angelic smile. A choir girl. "Yeah?"

"I didn't know you weren't feeling well. Do you need me to stay until six?"

"Well, I do have a little headache and I might also leave early, but don't worry about it. You go on to your interview."

"Tracy, that's not what I just heard. I got off the phone with Right Connections begging me to stay. Now, if you need me to stay, it's no problem at all—I swear. Just say the word and I'll stay."

"No, you can definitely go. Don't worry, I'll be all right."

"Are you sure, now? Because if there's any doubt at all..."

"Yes, I'm sure." She smiled broadly. "You can go...really."

"It's really okay? Because—"

"Listen," she said in a stern but friendly voice. "I'm telling you, it's all right. I wouldn't say it was all right if it wasn't. Now not another word on this."

She looked at me and smiled with total warmth, like a mother who has just reprimanded her son. I felt relieved. The head of personnel must have misunderstood. Tracy couldn't possibly have lied so convincingly. No one was *that* good—it would be too evil. Plus, I really needed to go on the interview.

Tracy left the office early, at four-thirty, with her usual two overstuffed canvas bags. A severe concussion could never stop Supergirl.

"Hey, feel better, Tracy!" I called out and grinned.

"Don't worry about me." She beamed at me with her Pepsodent smile. "And good luck on your interview!"

"Thanks." Maybe I had judged her unkindly after all.

I was lying in bed at ten-thirty in the morning, several days after my interviews with Alec Baldwin and Kim Basinger, feeling restless and bored. It was my second day in a row without a temp assignment. I grabbed the remote control and began channel surfing. I could find nothing more amusing than the ending of a *Joy of Painting* episode with Bob Ross, a white guy with a seventies-style Afro and a soothing voice. I always found him hypnotic.

"Let's build us today a happy little cloud. I'm gonna take a little titanium white right on the ol' two-inch brush. And let's go up in here and just drop in an indication of some little clouds that live up here...Wherever...It doesn't matter where...Wherever you think they should live; that's *exactly* where they should be." That's why I liked him; in Bob Ross's microcosm, you could do no wrong.

I followed that with a repeat episode of *Lifestyles of the Rich and Famous.* I displaced all brain waves for the moment and listened while Robin Leach described today's fabulous story of excess.

"His name is Adnan Khashoggi," the Englishman began in stentorian tones. "This multi-billionaire is at home in any one of his twelve fabulous homes in the world's most glamorous cities. Whether driving around in one of his eighteen Rolls-Royces or jetting the globe in one of his five custom-made jets, Adnan Khashoggi is a true cosmopolitan!

"His hilltop retreat overlooking the beach at Saint Tropez," he continued, his voice rising to a crescendo, "is worth a fabulous thirty-five million dollars!!"

I flicked the television off, comforting myself with the thought that if I had that kind of money, I would not flaunt it on national television.

The phone rang, and I lunged to answer it.

"I'm sorry, Everett." "We did what we could do." The Harriet and Pauline show.

"W-what are you talking about?"

"He doesn't know." "We better tell him."

"Tell me what?" I was starting to worry.

"Disney." "Tracy went ballistic."

I sat up in bed. "WHAT?"

"She called up the head of personnel yesterday and demanded that you be blacklisted from Disney." "We had no choice, Everett—it was either you or us."

"She did *what* now?"

"The head of personnel told us that either we blacklist you from future Disney temp assignments or we won't get any more Disney contracts." "They're our biggest client by far, you know."

I was sputtering with rage. "B-but you know that after we spoke she said it was okay to leave. I told her I'd stay, but she smiled at me and wished me luck. She practically ordered me to leave...Believe me, I wouldn't have left if she had told me to stay."

The Right Connections women were surprisingly supportive. "We know—it's not the first time she's given our temps trouble. She has a reputation." "We'll take care of you though. We'll have to keep you away from the creative side for now and see if we can work you into other areas at Disney."

"I can't believe this...it's—it's beyond evil."

"We know, honey." "Don't take it personally."

I hung up the phone, wanting to cry. I didn't even care that much about not being able to work at Disney. What enraged me was that Tracy, representative of many young people in Hollywood, was at least as mean as she was successful. Her beautiful facade hid her true disposition. I also couldn't stand the emasculating feeling of not being able to retaliate, utterly powerless in the face of such outrage. I wondered if Wells knew of Tracy's behavior outside of his presence and momentarily considered relating to him the whole episode.

The phone rang again later, while I was watching *Love Connection* in bed. Even though the sun was streaming through the window, I had nothing else to do that day and didn't feel like leaving the security of my bed. It was my mother, calling "just to see what's new." I was annoyed, more at myself for having nothing to reply.

"Well, for starters, I've just sold all my possessions and pledged my life and soul to the great Rajnish in Portland, Oregon."

She paused for several seconds, an art that all Jewish mothers must learn before having children. "You'll *beg* me to talk with you later."

Guilt washed over me and I sighed. "I'm sorry. Look, Ma, I was only kidding. It's just—" The call-waiting signal beeped. "Listen, I'll call you back in a couple of minutes, Mom. Love you."

"Is this Everett?" An unfamiliar young male voice.

"Yes?"

"Hi, this is Mike from Alec Baldwin's office."

"Hi, Mike." So you're the one he wanted to fire. I wondered if he knew that Alec had interviewed me to replace him.

"Hi...Are you available for a call from Alec?"

What did he mean available? "Yeah, sure...Is he on the line?"

"No. I'm just checking to make sure that you're in. We'll call you back in ten minutes."

Forty minutes passed.

"Hello, Everett?"

"Yes?"

"It's Mike again."

"Hi, Mike. How have you been?"

"Fine." No-nonsense kind of guy. "Hold on for Alec."

"Great, can't wait."

"I'll patch you through to his car phone."

The line went scratchy with static. "Hi, this is Alec Baldwin."

"Hi, Alec, it's Everett. I thought you were in Brazil with Kim." It was great to be on a first-name basis with the stars.

"We had to delay things a few days. I'm on my way to the airport now." Great, so I went through the fiasco with Tracy for nothing.

He paused, and static filled the line. "Listen, about the job, I haven't made up my mind either way, and I've got a lot of other things on my plate right now...But I wanted you to know that things are starting to gel between me and my assistant. If there's any change or anything, I'll call you right away."

"Gel?"

"Yeah, things are working out between the two of us right now."

"Hmmm...Sorry to hear that, actually."

"Yeah." He paused and then resumed in an end-of-conversation tone. "But, hey, I just want you to know that you were by far my first choice. Everyone was really impressed with you."

I swallowed. "Thanks." I suddenly had a brainstorm. "Hey, Alec, can you recommend anyone else I could call who's looking to hire right now?" I figured I had nothing to lose, and he did say that I was his number one choice.

"Uhhh...n-nothing comes to mind right now. But...let me think about that and, uh, I'll get back to you soon."

"Great...And maybe we'll run in to each other some day when I'm working at a studio." Yeah, and I'll mess with your life the way you did mine.

Barbara Dreyfus apologetically told me afterwards that every so often Baldwin threatened to fire his assistant, thus beginning another round of interviews with assistant hopefuls. And there was always some wannabe like me who got hyped by the process only to be dropped.

The rational side of me reasoned that Baldwin had technically done nothing wrong; it was his prerogative to hire or fire. My gut reaction, however, was to take great glee in the bad karma that soon came his way. His movie with Kim Basinger, *The Marrying Man*, one of Disney's big spring releases for 1991, was a flop at the box office and took a drubbing by critics. (*Variety* called it "a still-born romantic comedy of staggering ineptitude.") The movie's production costs were over $26 million, while the box office take was under $12 million. The press had a field day, with *Premiere* and *People* inflicting the most damage with tales from the set presenting Baldwin and Basinger as temperamental prima donnas. Then, Baldwin played tough in negotiations with Paramount over a starting date for the filming of *Patriot Games*, the second installment in the slated Tom Clancy film trilogy, so that he could appear on Broadway in the lead role of Stanley Kowalski opposite Jessica Lange as Blanche Dubois in a revival of Tennessee Williams's *A Streetcar Named Desire* (for which he would receive a Tony nomination). Paramount unceremoniously ditched Baldwin, who was to have received $4 million for the role, and hired Harrison Ford. The movie did just fine without him, grossing over $80 million in the United States and an additional $100 million worldwide. In the summer of 1994, Ford also starred in the third Clancy film, *Clear and Present Danger*, which grossed over $120 million domestically. Baldwin appeared that same summer in a critically panned remake of *The Shadow*.

The gods were not smiling at Kim Basinger, either. She was sued for breaking a verbal commitment to star in *Boxing Helena* after she resigned in 1991 before filming began. The producer, Carl Mazzocone, contended that this action cost the production millions in foreign presale rights and start-up costs. (I wondered why Basinger agreed in the first place to appear in a campy film about a surgeon who amputates the arms and legs of the woman he loves and keeps her in a box until she reciprocates his devotion. Not exactly a career-enhancing premise. Sherilyn Fenn eventually played the role, and the film grossed under $2 million.) After a prolonged trial, in March 1993 a Superior Court jury ordered Basinger to pay the producer $8.1 million in damages, which drove her into personal bankruptcy. After the decision, Mazzocone received a congratulatory phone call from Jeffrey Katzenberg, among others. (In September 1994, a California appeals court overturned the ruling because the jury had received improper instructions. That ruling sent the case back to the state trials court.) As for her Braselton project, her partner and unsecured creditor, Ameritech, auctioned off the Bank of Braselton and was trying to sell the rest of the town's real estate for less than half of what they paid.

Alec and Kim were married in the summer of 1993.

I was surprised to get a Disney post the following Monday after my conversation about Tracy's "blacklist" with Harriet and Pauline. Television finance, though, was far enough away from production, in terms of both location and milieu, for me to avoid running into Tracy.

As I drove to Burbank, I had this nagging feeling about television finance at Disney. It seemed familiar to me, but I couldn't remember why.

I walked through the brand-new Michael Graves–designed Team Disney building with the nineteen-foot-tall dwarfs carved into the upper floors' design (typical Disney: playful and fun on the outside masking the fear and terror inside). My footsteps echoed on the concrete floor as I walked through the inner courtyard, which was as dark and drafty as a dungeon. From what I had heard, the structure was a nightmare to work in.

I put my newspaper and pocket diary down at the secretary's desk and was relieved to see that the phone system was identical to Frank

Wells's. Suddenly, I spied a familiar face down the hallway. I did a classic double take, and it suddenly hit me. Will Keller worked in television finance at Disney! My friend Alexandra had been a classmate of his at Harvard Business School and had advised me to look him up when I moved westward; we had gone out drinking together on a number of occasions. Well, isn't that special? I was to be a secretary to a fellow MBA—and from Harvard at that.

I plastered a smile on my face as Keller came by to greet me. He didn't quite know how to handle it either. Thankfully, he introduced me to his colleagues as if I were visiting on a job interview and not there to answer phones and type memos. "Peter, Ted, Tom, this is Everett Weinberger from New York. He's a Stanford MBA, class of '90 and Columbia undergrad, '86." Oh Will, you forgot that I also make a great cup of coffee and type fifty words a minute.

Working there gave me the chance to see what life would have been like for me had I gotten a traditional finance position at a studio. It was just as I had surmised after my summer experience in finance at Paramount. There was nothing inherently fascinating about what these guys were doing vis-à-vis their counterparts at a consumer products company or at a ball bearing manufacturer.

This row of offices was extremely quiet throughout the day. No rapid-fire phone calls, no eccentric producers rushing in and out, no slamming doors or thrown books. It was like almost any office in corporate America: pleasant, predictable, and boring. Just the sounds of computer keys, turning pages, and hushed conversations, and the definite feeling that more important events were taking place outside of these offices.

But the Disney finance crew did get to drive through the studio gates every day and were able to tell people outside of the industry that they worked at Disney, which to the uninitiated sounded cool. Plus, as Will told me, they got super discounts at Disney-owned resorts and stores. As if that would compensate them for the long hours and lousy pay: $10 off every time they visited Disneyland!

Will also explained to me the office furniture hierarchy at Disney.

As you rose in title, you also qualified for better quality furniture. The mere existence of a couch in one's office signified a senior level at Disney. Furthermore, the type of couch—its size, material, and quality—allowed Will to pinpoint the exact level of the executive.

The main project Will was working on was a computer model that calculated the probabilities of various payout scenarios for the Disney-produced game shows, allowing them to more accurately budget the prize money. Most of the other MBAs on the lot worked in strategic planning and development, headed by Lawrence Murphy, a former consultant who functioned as chief of staff for Eisner, Wells, and other top Disney managers. His finance gang, mostly expatriates from prestigious consulting firms and investment banks, crunched the numbers for potential acquisitions and new ventures. These people calculated ingenious ways to save the studio thousands of dollars each month while the production executives figured out equally creative ways to waste millions. I was still sure I'd rather be with the ones spending than those saving.

I kept feeling that Will was trying to put in a good word for me with his boss, as if I were interning there for a finance job. Still, he meant well; he was so bewildered at seeing me at his secretary's desk that he refrained from asking me to do any menial tasks.

We even ate lunch together each day, the temp and the executive. Walking with Will to the commissary along Mickey Avenue, the main street on the lot, I felt rather carefree, dressed in casual clothes and wearing sunglasses, as if I were the creative artist and he were the "suit" from accounting. And at the commissary, I knew more people than Will did, through all my temp jobs and interviews. Rita even dropped by with some beautiful D-girls and executive assistants, which impressed Will, especially when he learned that Rita worked for Spock. Funny how I had seen much more of the studio and Hollywood while temping than Will had in his permanent job at Disney—proof that who you knew in Hollywood was still more important than what you knew.

CHAPTER 14

The Next Generation

*Experience is not what happens to a man; it is what
a man does with what happens to him.*

ALDOUS HUXLEY

Flush with some discretionary income from temping, I began dedicating myself more seriously to the L.A. social scene. Aside from going out to bars and clubs with Anton or Mitch, I attended the occasional charity or film party. I wasn't invited to nor could I afford the fund-raisers for the political causes most in vogue in Hollywood. That was fine with me, as I didn't have to listen to Barbra Streisand or Susan Sarandon pontificate on AIDS or U.S. foreign policy, as well as on the responsibility of celebrities to "get involved."

No, I went out solely to meet women. I still nursed the fantasy that I would meet a gorgeous California girl who would make me a part of the in crowd. I was also desperate for some female company (my thing with Deirdre had fizzled out from its own inertia).

Anton, as usual, got me the invitation to a charity function that sounded like it might be fun. It was to be held in Santa Monica at the

Fifth Avenue restaurant, an auspicious name to an ex–New Yorker. The admission price was a toy, which would be donated to the poor children who lived in L.A., though you never actually saw them unless you took the wrong turn off the freeway or watched the evening news.

I entered the crowded restaurant and dropped a Bart Simpson doll onto a sprawling pile of toys, dismayed that there were no fewer than five others already there. Amstel Light in hand, I stood at the bar and munched on some peanut M&Ms, looking at the door to see if Anton was going to show. With nothing better to do, I sauntered around the bar, nodding and smiling to no one in particular.

One great annoyance for me at these social events was the inevitable "What do you do?" True, it came later in the conversation than in New York, where it was usually the opening query, but it nonetheless was always asked. I hated to lie, and initially I would launch into a song and dance about how I was an MBA interviewing to become a production executive but was only temping at the time. After one woman made a face, said, "Oh, another wannabe," and abruptly turned her back on me, I decided it might be advisable to modify the response. Thus, the temp job I was currently in became my current position. It was much simpler and close enough to the truth.

I spotted three women in animated conversation and ambled over to listen.

"God, you'd think they had found a way in this city to manufacture perfect human bodies," said a woman in her mid-thirties in a loud New York accent. "I mean, just look at these women." She gestured at a group of Barbie-doll women at the bar. "I'll bet there's a law in L.A. that if you're over a size six, they ship you north to San Francisco!"

At last, a woman with a sense of humor. I turned to join them. "I know what you mean," I said. "I *hate* when women have perfect bodies!"

She laughed and cocked her head at me. "Sarcasm? Do I detect New York sarcasm?"

"You certainly do. Do I detect intelligent life forms?"

"Absolutely. So, should I be a typical New Yorker and ask what you do right away, or act like a Californian and weasel the question in after an hour? Actually, I've already asked, so I can't retract it."

"Since you're obviously fresher to L.A. than me, why don't you begin?"

"Oh, I like the attitude—real gutsy. Well, at least you're not like these gorgeous but brain-dead L.A. men. Okay, let's begin again." She shook my hand firmly. "My name's Felice Russell, and, as you guessed, I just moved here from the City—I assume I don't have to define which city. I'm a financial journalist who's in the midst of a full-blown mid-career crisis. I freelance for the *Economist, Euromoney, Institutional Investor,* and other business-type magazines. I write about fascinating things like index options and Eurobonds. Anyway, to make a long story short, I came to La-La Land to check out this whole movie business thing and see whether and where I can fit in."

Good Lord, I thought. This industry must be heading for collapse, like Wall Street in the eighties, when people like her move here. Felice was the antithesis of the prototypical L.A. woman: pudgy, over thirty, intellectual, and sharply cynical. I couldn't imagine someone less likely to make it in motion picture development.

"Welcome to the movie carnival!" I said. "And congratulations, you're the millionth New Yorker to move here this month. We have some special door prizes for you." She laughed. "But really, it's great to have another kindred soul here."

I explained to her what I was doing in L.A. and related some of my experiences during the last year, trying to accentuate the positive, as I didn't want to scare her. We talked for several hours, and, uncharacteristically, I barely paid attention to the MAWs (models-actresses-whatevers) at the party. Though I had no interest in Felice romantically, she was a welcome relief from the standard fare I usually met at these parties. Just to converse with an intelligent person about topics other than the movie industry was a delight. The industry was so insular and self-absorbed that I often forgot how trivial the film business was to the outside world.

In the weeks after the party, Felice became my student of sorts, and frequently called me for counsel on how to run the gauntlet of Hollywood obstacles. I was glad, for her sake, to hear that ultimately she wanted to write screenplays. After all, writers in Hollywood did not have to look stylish. In fact, creative executives *expected* writers to be cynical East Coast intellectuals.

I had also recently considered writing a "spec script" (a completed script as opposed to a proposal or a pitch) and then finding an agent who would peddle it around town. After all, hadn't I learned the standard three-act script structure by writing coverage and notes on lots of scripts? And who could ignore the headlines in *Variety* touting spec scripts like Shane Black's *The Last Boy Scout* and Joe Eszterhaus's *Basic Instinct,* which had recently sold for $1.75 million and $3 million, respectively? (Black eventually broke Eszterhaus's record in 1994 when he sold *The Long Kiss Goodnight* for $4 million.)

The story making the rounds at the time was that a local television station had set up a minicam on a street corner in L.A. and asked random passersby, "So, how's your screenplay coming along?" The majority of people responded, "Fine," or "So-so," or "How did you know?" Construction workers, delivery boys, and cashiers alike all paused to talk about their big project.

After spending months calling on industry insiders to ask for something, the thought of having agents, producers, and development executives wining and dining me was alluring. But it wasn't like I had a passionate urge to tell a story. It was merely another way to score in the Hollywood fame and fortune game I was intent on winning. I was considering every other option, so why not writing? I realized that this attitude was part of the vicious cycle that led to formulaic movies in Hollywood: So many mediocre screenplays are made into films, that many writers figure they can do no worse, and most succeed in doing just that.

I went as far as to outline the plots of several potential screenplays. I also met with Sid Newman, my friend Neil's childhood friend who was now a screenwriter and had sold several unproduced scripts for ludicrous sums.

He picked me up in his brand-new Cadillac convertible, complete with note pad on the dashboard and microcassette recorder. "Just in case I come up with multi-million-dollar ideas on the freeway," he said, matter-of-factly.

Newman wore wire-rimmed glasses and a black baseball cap which read, WHITE MEN CAN'T JUMP, given to the cast and crew of the film. T-shirts, caps, and jackets from the latest productions were status symbols in L.A., especially if you weren't involved with the film.

We talked over lunch at Johnny Rocket's, a fifties-style diner on Melrose. Right away, I learned that screenwriters are not necessarily from the same breed as novelists. "Tell me, Sid, why do you prefer to write scripts rather than books?"

He snorted. "Get real—I could easily write books. But I can crank out a script in a few weeks and make like ten times as much. It's just a matter of opportunity cost—it's that simple."

"But don't you ever want to write something with literary depth?"

"Fuck literary!" he said, as he bit into his cheeseburger. "It's all about cash flow. I can't afford to wait for like a year to write a book and another year to find a publisher and another year for it to be published. I can write like God knows how many scripts in that time, you know? Fact is, most of my income doesn't even come from original spec scripts. It comes from assignments like rewrites or rewrites of rewrites. I'm just like a hired gun most of the time." His current literary endeavor was an assignment to write a movie version of the cartoon series *Speed Racer*.

Despite how easy this guy made it sound, the more I worked in development offices, the more I saw the frustrations screenwriters faced. Even if they were successful enough to get a script into development at a studio (itself an awesome achievement), they had to undergo rewrite after rewrite, or "development hell," only to see their project languish for lack of momentum. Other than the ten top screenwriters, writers had no authority over their scripts and were not regarded as so talented that they could not be fired for any one of ten thousand other eager writers.

I met Felice for brunch one Sunday in late December at Penny Feathers in West Hollywood, a down-to-earth restaurant whose location at the busy corner of La Cienega and Melrose afforded some of L.A.'s best people-watching, or at least car-watching. Felice wanted me to help her chart out a networking plan of attack. I also offered to share with her my notebook filled with names and phone numbers of contacts. She was dressed in a black turtleneck and jeans even though it was over eighty degrees outside.

"Uhh...nice outfit, Felice. Going skiing any time soon?"

"I know, I know, not very stylish. But honestly, I'm always cold in this city. I mean, all I do is move from one air-conditioned environment to another. Plus, I still haven't gotten around to buying new outfits. All I have is my New York manic-depressive line of clothing. And given my current bank balance, I don't think I'll be heading to Versace any time soon. Do you know if Ikea sells clothing too? God, I love that store!"

There was something very comfortable and familiar about Felice, like a favorite pair of jeans. I could talk with her for hours without tiring and with no pretense. I saw myself in Felice, only eight months before (me, a veteran!). As she fired questions at me about the industry and job hunting, I felt flattered to be the "expert" giving out advice after being on the receiving end for so long.

After brunch, we strolled south along La Cienega Boulevard toward the Beverly Center shopping mall. We were the only two figures on the sidewalk. It was a surrealistic scene as we slowly walked in the scorching sun along this commercial corridor and did not pass another soul. I felt like an explorer of another planet, an alien. And these metal creatures with wheels flashed by us in both directions without stopping. I knew right then that I could never feel at home in a city where walking was a lost art form.

We entered the mall and window-shopped, each homesick for the traditional Christmas atmosphere in New York. You didn't have to celebrate Christmas to appreciate the holiday spirit in Manhattan. The wreaths, the colored lights, and the Christmas carols wafting through the mall did not jibe with the air-conditioning and people in shorts and tank tops. I kept thinking of Woody Allen in *Annie Hall*, commenting sarcastically on the fake atmosphere of Christmas in L.A. It was apropos, since the Beverly Center was where Allen and Bette Midler had filmed *Scenes From a Mall*.

We leaned over a balcony and watched the Christmas display. A lone piano player clad in a red and black smoking jacket played holiday favorites on a white grand piano. Santa Claus was there in traditional red garb and white beard, ready to pose with children for photographs—that much was familiar. But two of Santa's voluptuous blond helpers with low-cut outfits and black high-heeled boots were also available for glossy five-by-eights. Now that was a Yuletime feature I wouldn't have minded seeing back east.

I arrived at home later that day and listened to a long message from the woman whose apartment I was subletting, without a lease, on a month-to-month basis. In my buoyant optimism eight months prior,

I had imagined graduating by now to a better apartment. I had also assumed that this apartment would be available indefinitely. Wrong. Very apologetically, she told me she was returning in one week and expected me to vacate by then.

That weekend, I rented a small U-Haul truck and moved north to Mitch's father's house in Woodland Hills, the heart of the San Fernando Valley (or just "the Valley" to residents). This was true suburbia in all its glory: expansive four-lane avenues lined with drive-thru fast-food restaurants and car dealerships, one after the other, repeating again every half mile. You could rip out the entire downtown and place it in Akron or Stamford and it would blend right in.

I have never felt more beholden to anyone than to Mitch and his father for taking me and my possessions in from the heat. I have never been good at asking for and taking favors from people. (My father always ingrained in us the "Neither a borrower nor lender be" axiom.) I was filled with self-pity at times, as I sat eating spaghetti dinners with the two of them.

While at Mitch's, I was also at a near standstill in both my job search and temp jobs. It was the period immediately before and after New Year's when the industry was at its lowest ebb, even though, ironically, this was the second-busiest moviegoing time of the year (the summer season was still the industry's annual juggernaut, accounting for 40 percent of the year's box office gross). The trades were skimpier than usual, as most executives shipped off to Hawaii or Aspen.

I stayed at their house during the day while Mitch and his father went off to work (my breadwinners). When repairmen or deliverymen came to the house, I felt like some bored 1950s suburban housewife. But, unlike New York where the cold drives people indoors in January, in the Valley it was always sunny outside, and I couldn't bear to while away the day indoors watching television. I jogged often in the blazing heat on the gleaming tar roads, feeling like the last man on earth as I ran past the sprinkler-abetted lawns and the empty, near-identical houses. Or I lounged around the backyard pool (less a luxury in the Valley than a necessity) with their two German shepherds keeping me company. I discovered why many people talk to their dogs—not because they think the dogs will understand, but out of desire for companionship.

Finally, in late January I found a small but well-situated apartment on the outskirts of Beverly Hills. Located at 915½ South Holt Avenue, it was above a four-car garage (hence the ½—whenever another unit was added to a house in Los Angeles, the new dwelling added ½, ¼, or even ⅛ to the original address). Rent was $550 a month, which would have been a bargain when I was living in New York, but was now barely within my means. Plus, I had no furniture of my own, other than a futon, a card table, and a wastebasket.

I spent one Sunday afternoon debating for hours about signing the lease. While working out at Gold's Gym, I played out the arguments in my mind. On the one hand, I kept hearing Harvey Shulman, the Columbia creative executive: "You've gotta give it at least a year, maybe two or three." Counterbalancing that argument was my father, of course, with the oft-heard "You must be out of your freakin' mind!"

What swayed me to stay was my fear of losing. I was committed big-time to this course of action, especially since everyone I knew was expecting me to become a Hollywood big shot. If I left now, I would be admitting failure, which my ego refused to consider.

"Snap out of it!" Felice said after I had spent five minutes over breakfast one morning complaining to her about the lack of direction in my life and the doubts I was having about staying in L.A. We were seated in a booth at Kate Mantilini's, a stylish diner on Wilshire. For the price of a muffin and coffee (albeit an exorbitantly priced muffin and coffee), we could sit amidst the hubbub of deal-making agents.

"Don't you want to hear about my Robert McKee marathon? I am so charged up—I feel like holing myself up in my apartment and not coming out until I finish my screenplay." Felice had spent Friday through Sunday the weekend before enrolled in the famed Robert McKee Story Structure course. For three days, she sat and listened to the wisdom of self-professed screenwriting guru Robert McKee, who packed his seminars with screenwriter and creative executive wannabes at $400 a head. It was no accident that Hollywood films and the standard three-act structure were becoming even more ingrained and formulaic. The old axiom "Practice makes permanent" was very much in evidence in Hollywood scriptwriting.

I smiled at her and affected an old Jewish man's voice. "Oy, Felice. I really envy you. Ven I vas a younger man, I too had my dreams. I too thought that the voild vas my oyster. I only vish I had your enthusiasm and optimism." I was only half kidding. I often felt like a cynical veteran who had seen too much.

"Listen, I know that Cancers are sensitive to criticism..." One of Felice's flakier attributes was that she was heavily into astrology. "Especially those born in your year, but here goes my two cents. I think you've got to stop moping around and whining, and start taking some proactive steps regarding your career. I know you're going to think I'm batty, but I know a tarot card reader—"

"Oh God..." I held my hands over my head in mock despair. "Is that what my life has come to? I can just see my father: 'Sylvia, the boy has finally flipped out!'"

She held up her hand. "Forget about your father for once! Just hold on and hear me out. She's based in Brecksville, Ohio—don't ask me where that is—and she reads your future over the phone. Everett, she's really excellent at it. I've called her many times and referred her to some friends who also swear by her—and these are professionals who were nonbelievers like you. I just think calling her might help you see things more clearly."

"CALL HER?"

"Shhh. Keep your voice down." We looked around us at the

creative executive types having power breakfasts who flicked their eyes at us.

I hunched over the table and whispered. "Are you trying to tell me that you pay some woman you've never seen in Ohio to read your fortune over the phone for you? That's crazy! I mean, if you're into card-reading, why not go in person to someone local in L.A.?"

"I know it sounds weird. But if you're tuned in and have the gift, you can channel someone from anywhere, and she's incredibly accurate. She once told me I was going to lose one freelance writing assignment in New York I wanted very badly and get another one in London, which I hadn't even known about at the time. Of course, it happened exactly that way. I like her because she's not afraid to stick her neck out and tell you what's going to happen. You really should call her, and you should do it in the next few weeks. My friend told me she's eight months pregnant now, so she's in a heightened state of awareness."

"Heightened state of awareness, huh? Well, how much does this heightened state of awareness cost?"

"Forty dollars for a half hour, plus she mails you a tape of the session."

"Well why didn't you say so? At that price, I'll be calling her two, three times a day, at least." I couldn't hold my serious expression and broke into a smile.

Felice playfully punched me in the arm and handed me the psychic's business card, which I filed in my wallet next to my expired Stanford parking permit and other unlikely-to-be-used-again items.

I soon forgot about Felice's advice and landed some steady temp assignments, principally in the marketing department at Disney home video. I also spent several days at Gallin-Morey Associates, which sounded like a law firm but was in fact a well-known management firm run by Sandy Gallin and Jim Morey. I was the front-desk receptionist—you know, the bored-looking woman you typically see when the elevator opens. It was fun, though—since I answered every call that came in through the main number. I got to say "Please hold" to as many callers as I cared to.

From the mail delivered to the firm, I soon learned that the management team handled Dolly Parton, Michael Jackson, Neil Diamond, and Sandra Bernhard. In fact, I had visited these offices seven months earlier when I met with producer Howard Rosenman, who with Dolly Parton and Gallin were co-heads of Sandollar Productions.

Sandy Gallin was a well-known manager, as much for his close friends, such as Barry Diller and David Geffen, as for his clients, both present and past. A former agent, he had helped manage the careers of Whoopi Goldberg, Cher, Barbra Streisand, Lily Tomlin, Richard Pryor, Olivia Newton-John and the Pointer Sisters. As far as I could tell, personal managers ranked somewhere on the Hollywood food chain alongside the agent, the lawyer, the publicist, and the business manager. They essentially functioned as the star's best friend, shaping the career and doling out commonsensical advice. Personal managers often developed and produced projects for their clients. If you had enough money, it seemed, it was de rigueur to have one.

I amused myself during my stint there by reading the stacks of opened fan letters. Particularly high in humor content were the letters waiting to be forwarded to clients Milli Vanilli. The singers had recently admitted that they had not sung any of the hit songs on their best-selling "Girl You Know It's True" album. I chuckled as I read letters from thirteen-year-old girls from the United States, Jamaica, and Europe, all pledging their undying love, devotion, and support for the beleaguered lip-syncers. "I don't care what they say or what lies they tell about you—I'll always believe you sang those songs!"

Howard Rosenman walked by several times before I got up the courage to reintroduce myself. The producer's eyes registered recognition, but he didn't say more than, "Oh, hi," before scurrying back to his desk. I guess my status as the temporary receptionist answered the question how I was doing.

I settled into a routine of single-day temp assignments, and the next few weeks passed in a blur. Then, several events shattered the calm.

At first I didn't recognize the pretty blonde sitting alone in the nearly empty Jack in the Box restaurant, but I knew I'd met her somewhere. I was bleary-eyed tired that Friday night from a week's worth of temping in the television commercial sales department at local station KTLA, and in no mood to think about what to eat, so I had allowed myself the cheap luxury of fast food. I was so hungry that I didn't even bother looking for a restaurant with a drive-thru window.

"Fries, filet of fish, Diet Coke and...that'll be it. To go, please." I glanced behind me again, my eyes focusing now on the blonde, her hair tied in a neat ponytail, an overstuffed tan canvas bag beside her. Tracy Sure-You-Can-Leave-Early Taylor! Good God! Alone, on a Friday night, hunched over a soggy burger in an antiseptic Jack in the Box on Santa Monica Boulevard. With a gentle look on her face, she barely resembled the Doberman who had barked at me so viciously.

Unconsciously, I pulled out bills and handed them to the cashier, my body turned sideways so I could continue watching her. Here was a portrait of the wannabe. No outsider who envisioned the career path of a movie executive would ever stop and consider the nights I, Tracy, and many other hopefuls spent in places like this.

I had built her up in my mind as a monster, and yet, seeing her in the vulnerable state, I forgave Tracy at that moment. Should I go over and talk to her? No, I decided. She'd be sure to resurrect her defenses and proffer some excuse for being there. She'd have said that she was doing top-secret research on fast-food chains for Frank. Then I'd hate her all over again. Instead, I grabbed my bag and headed home.

Hearing the phone ring in my apartment as I got out of my car, I raced up the stairs, fumbling with my keys. I dropped my packages on the floor and lunged for the phone. The line clicked and beeped as I answered, indicating an overseas call. Who could be calling me at this hour from abroad?

"Hey dude, guess who?"

"Anton! What's going on? Where are you calling from?"

"I'm in London, Ev," he said, leisurely pausing to inhale a cigarette, "and it's absolutely amazing here."

"Geez, it must be past two in the morning there."

"Actually, it's past three," he said gleefully, drinking something. "I just got back from the clubs."

"I didn't know you were taking vacation now. I thought you were just in Hawaii, or someplace."

"I was and I'm not. Actually, this has happened quite quickly, so I didn't call you until now. I've been transferred to McKinsey London. Basically, L.A. is passé anyway. It's been that way for the last few months. But you should see the buzz in the air here. You've got to get over here soon."

"But what about Kristie?" I asked dumbly. I should have asked "But what about me?" given that Anton was one of the best friends I had in L.A.

"Well, she's going to come over next month using my frequent flier miles. Besides, there's more where she came from—especially in Paris. You should see the talent there."

"But I thought you loved L.A. I mean, you owned this city."

"Don't get me wrong—L.A. was a cool place to live after b-school. But I had a great opportunity in the London office and I took it—you'd have done the same. Also, I kind of miss my family in Europe and wanted to be closer to them."

Yikes! Anton, who did so well in L.A., who was the embodiment of L.A., was moving on with his life. He was doing what was best for himself. And the king of philanderers was actually giving priority to his family.

I pulled out the fries and sandwich from the bag, turned on the television, and prepared to engage in my nightly ritual of dinner and TV. The phone rang again and, frowning, I grabbed the receiver, ready to cut short any conversation.

"Hey, Everett, it's Neil... KEEP IT DOWN, GUYS! I'm calling to give you the chance to wish me happy birthday." I could hear the cacophony of bar sounds: jukebox music, glasses, laughter, loud voices.

I smiled, picturing my friends in New York in some bar on the Upper West Side. "Hey, that's right! Happy birthday, Neil! What's that, twenty-seven? Getting up there, old man!"

"Thanks a lot—you're not too far behind yourself, you know."

"Where are you guys anyway—Lucy's?"

"Lucy's? That place hasn't been good for years. No, we're at a new place called Hi Life on Amsterdam."

"YO, EV, THIS ONE'S FOR YOU!" a voice slurred into the phone.

"Give me that! That was Jeff, like you couldn't tell... Hey, we miss you here. It's not the same without you."

A lump the size of Rhode Island appeared in my throat. "I miss you guys too, believe me... not that things aren't great here or anything. But I think it would be fun to come back to New York and hang out with you guys."

"You're such a kidder. We were just talking about the wild times you must be having out there. You're probably on your way out to party with Michelle Pfeiffer." They still preferred fantasy to reality.

"Yeah, something like that," I said, eyeing my lukewarm fish sandwich. "Hey, Neil, tell me something... I hear so much crap about New York out here. Is it really as dirty and cold and bad as I hear?"

"What the hell are you talkin' about? Of course it's dirty and cold. But it's still fuckin' great!"

I slowly hung up the phone and half-heartedly munched on my now-cold fish sandwich and fries while watching *Entertainment Tonight*, the Rolls Royce of industry gossip shows. Suddenly, I needed quiet and turned off the television. I sat at the card table in the kitchen, the one overhead bulb lighting the room, put my hands over my face, and moaned.

Tracy, Anton, Neil. My past was telling me I had to change my present. I knew each episode had some deeper meaning, but I pushed these thoughts aside. I didn't want to spend time psychoanalyzing them. Nor did I want to spend the time creating a decision tree, an analytical tool we had studied in business school that was supposed to facilitate decision-making. I found that these diagrams just made me all the more confused and disheartened over how many damned decisions I had to make.

No, I just wanted someone to tell me which path I ought to take; I wanted to see a glimpse of the future. I searched through my papers and found the business card Felice had given me. "Sharon A. Klingler, Metaphysician. Starbringer Center. Psychic Consultations. Lectures. Past Life Therapy." Forty dollars, or four hours of temp work. Well, I figured that wasn't too much for peace of mind. And maybe the psychic would help me develop a new strategy for my stalled job search. I phoned her office the next morning and got an appointment for the following Monday.

"I feel a male and a female around you," the psychic began after I read my Visa card number to her assistant. "One I feel had problems in the lower part of the torso before he or she passed. I'm getting queasy in the stomach as if some treatment was bothering him or her. Are you able to identify these people in spirit older than you? Do you recognize the symptoms for anyone that passed away from your grandparents' generation?"

"Well...ummm...my mother's mother did have stomach cancer," I said uncomfortably. Maybe there was something to this.

"I'll go with her, with grandma. Bless her for coming. She holds a brand new coin, a penny, shiny and new. She takes her arm and crosses it over the horizon. This penny is something on your mind, something new you're doing in business. It's something you're focusing on now. Are you able to identify what this is, please?"

"Well...I recently completed business school, and this past eight months I've been in L.A. exploring a career in entertainment, and I've been wondering whether I should continue with it." I stopped myself from telling her more.

I heard sounds of cards being shuffled. I wondered if they were tarot cards or just ordinary playing cards—maybe she was playing solitaire and reading from a script. Could my skepticism spoil the reading?

"Okay, I've turned over the cards. In the twelfth house of your karma is the ace of pentacles or the hand holding one penny." She laughed—must have been some inside joke for psychics. "So, the cards are confirming what spirit said. Your next karmic cycle is the new beginning of your career life. You've got the fifth house of Leo, also the house of creativity: artist, actor, entertainment. I also see the knight of pentacles, which is the lawyer, negotiating, wheeling and dealing. Was there any of this energy in your search?"

"Y-yes, early on in my search I was torn between the creative side and the business side." Either she was good, or she was merely taking what I had told her and applying tarot cards' lingo to it.

"Well, the knights are all action, and pentacles are all business. It's mostly on the business side. I do have to tell you also, you have a lot of major arcana...you could go a lot of different places." What the heck were arcana?

"That's my problem in a nutshell—too many choices."

"In the eighth house of your transformation, you have the seven of wands reversed, which means trying to handle so many things you're losing control." She giggled and I envisioned two twenty-dollar bills with wings flying by. "And you have the wheel of fortune, which is the major arcanum of karma, in the ninth house. Now, the wheel of fortune represents being on your karmic path and finding all the places you're supposed to be—being on the right path." She paused. "As I tune in to one of them, has there been any interest by you in the banking or finance industry?"

I laughed. "That's funny, because that's where I came from—from investment banking."

"That makes sense, because the card shows a picture of dualistic energy. The woman's got a sword in each hand and a blindfold, so rather than trying to make a decision, she crosses the swords at her heart and puts a blindfold on herself so she doesn't have to deal with it. At this moment in time, you're not in a real strong position to make a decision about this. But I want to talk about the duality here. As I tune into one of the swords, I'm definitely getting a financial industry kind of thing, and the other one points to the creative industries. So, even though you've put that aside, I don't think you have really. That's why you're in such a quandary here. There's a part of you that hasn't totally let go of the financial industry."

"Interesting." I felt goose bumps on my arms and neck. Amazingly, she had zeroed in on my two areas of interest. Maybe there was something to this bullshit.

"You've also got the ten of wands, which is the card of moving from one city to the next, in the tenth house or the circle of the present, which means in the next three to six months."

"Wait a minute—what does that mean?"

"I definitely see you switching cities during the next two months." Whoa! Not only had she pinpointed the most gut-wrenching dilemma in my life, she was foretelling that I would leave L.A. for New York.

I lay in bed that night, trying to sort out my feelings toward L.A. and Hollywood. With my savings nearly gone, the temp jobs barely covering my expenses, and the value of my MBA in the corporate world steadily declining, I needed to make a decision.

Ironically, I had finally begun to get job offers as assistant to various production executives. It was usually left up to me to call them back if I was still interested in the job. That was the way I had left it with Stephanie Allain, a thirty-year-old rising star at Columbia Pictures who was one of the few black production executives in the industry. Articulate and intelligent, she was recognized for having championed writer/director John Singleton and his acclaimed *Boyz N the Hood*. I liked her, but I had seen all too well through Tracy and Brad what these positions entailed. Furthermore, her departing assistant pointed out to me the near impossibility at Columbia of moving directly to a creative executive post. She complained about the nepotism that was rampant at Columbia, with various relatives and friends of Guber and Peters installed in production positions.

Beyond the questionable desirability of these entry level jobs, it was becoming clear that I was not cut out to live in a city of freeways. Maybe, with family and friends and a girlfriend in town, I could have stuck it out. But it seemed patently easier to be engaged in a job search in New York than in L.A. Furthermore, Los Angeles, where every other car seemed to be a Porsche or Mercedes, was simply not a town for losers. The spoils of wealth were too openly displayed and respected for the have-nots to be content with their lot. Many wannabes lingered on in L.A. because the wealth seemed so tantalizingly obtainable. I preferred to be in Manhattan, for at least there the signs of wealth were often masked or stowed behind closed doors.

But aside from the great L.A. versus New York debate, I was beginning to believe that in order to succeed in Hollywood, I was going to have to mutate and become more like its entertainment industry denizens. I had already seen glimpses of how I might have to behave, and I didn't like what I saw. The schmoozing, the lying, the tongue-lashing. If I didn't like my character as a wannabe, I could only imagine how much worse I'd be as a full-fledged member of the Hollywood community.

I no longer believed that I would or could be any better or nicer than the executives I'd seen up close. And I realized that I didn't want to change and reinvent myself as so many out-of-towners had in Hollywood. My occasional outings with Anton and Kristie notwithstanding, this boy from Brooklyn had no desire to hide from his past nor to claim an L.A. identity as his own.

As I considered my options, faces of various people I had met during my search in L.A. flashed through my mind: David Kirkpatrick, Brad Dorman, Murray Krupnick, Nick Stevens, Alec Baldwin, Tracy Taylor. Each represented an important piece in a jigsaw puzzle whose image I was beginning to discern. No amount of rationalization could counteract my feelings: negative, negative, negative. Virtually all my experiences in this city had been negative. Either I had experienced colossally bad luck, or I had been given a taste of the bigger meal to come.

By two in the morning, I was beginning to reach a consensus from the various voices in my mind screaming their opinions and observations. I harked back to the momentous sleepless evening nearly three years before that had shifted my gaze westward. Coming full circle, I was now certain that it was time to move back east.

I just had to face down my feelings of failure and reassure myself that I could resurrect my career goals in New York. To be sure, there were far fewer entertainment-related companies there. The television networks were based in New York, though they were downsizing as their market share of the TV audience continued to fall. HBO was also in the city, and there were several independent film production companies in Manhattan, which struck me as my best options.

The next day, I felt as if the proverbial monkey had been lifted from my back; I had a restored sense of purpose, and with celerity I began making moving arrangements, which quickly snowballed and made the move self-fulfilling. My landlord was surprisingly understanding when I told him I had to break the lease after only a month. I think he always suspected this would occur, given how starkly I had furnished the flat. It was amazing how transient my life had become; I was able to pack up all my worldly possessions in three hours.

Rather than spend my last evening in L.A. alone in my barren apartment, I arranged to meet Mitch at Gorky's, a cafeteria in Hollywood that served inexpensive, hearty Russian fare and home-brewed beer (their slogan was catchy: "Foodski, funski, brewski"). I drove my trusty Corolla, which had served me well these past three years, along Sunset Boulevard.

I was lost in thought about my move and the uncertainties that awaited me. I was also distracted by the massive billboards trumpeting upcoming movie releases that lined "Sunset Strip," the section of Sunset Boulevard between Crescent Heights and Doheny Drive. Given the propensity of entertainment industry executives to drive along this avenue each day, these billboards were extremely valuable promotional tools (and at a cost of $10,000 to $20,000 a month were probably the most expensive billboards in the world). Fourteen feet high and forty-eight feet wide, they were difficult to ignore. My eyes were riveted to them, and I zoned out, unaware that I was driving anymore. (This phenomenon of being able to drive at high speeds and simultaneously daydream for minutes was both fascinating and terrifying to me whenever I caught myself at it.)

I snapped back to reality as a red BMW suddenly appeared in my front windshield, growing in size as I rapidly approached it. I jammed on my brakes, turned the wheel, and braced for the inevitable and sickening crunch of metal. CRASH! After several minutes of settling insurance matters with the other driver, I took notice that his car had little more than scratches, while my Toyota, with its scrunched-up grill, would clearly need to be junked.

The next day, my last in L.A., I picked up my car, which I had parked on a side street near Gorky's. Thankfully, it was still barely driveable, though it made an agonizing metal-screeching noise. I drove to Rent-a-Wreck, where I sold it for $150. The owner was sympathetic and lent me a battered Chevy station wagon for my last day in town. I was actually choked up as I looked back and saw the Corolla in the lot, parked among other beat-up autos. I couldn't help but feel like the car was a symbol of my stay in Los Angeles. Wrecking and selling it seemed a cathartic form of closure for me.

I stopped to pick up Felice, who had volunteered to drive me to the airport and return the car. First, we drove downtown to the Greyhound package center, where I was shipping two bulky items too large for UPS. The clerk weighed the packages, my bicycle and futon. As he processed the order, I looked at the row of packages lining the gray metallic shelves behind him. HUMAN EYES—HANDLE WITH CARE! was written on one styrofoam package in big block letters. It is a great country where you can ship bicycles alongside body organs.

With Felice in tow, the psychic experience fresh in my mind, and the fragile nature of my psyche, I tried to conjure up the cosmic connection between my move and this package of eyes. While waiting for the clerk, I pondered this Talmud-like riddle. The only answer I could come up with was that greater forces were watching and approving my move, and would be guiding it. Either that or someone heaven-sent was advising me to keep an "eye out" for my possessions on Greyhound and check "yes" to the extra insurance!

CHAPTER 15

Back to the Future

*Hate New York City—it's cold and it's damp. And all
the people dress like monkeys.*

RANDY NEWMAN, "I Love L.A."

*When it is good, New York is very good. Which is
why New Yorkers put up with so much that is bad.*

ADA LOUISE HUXTABLE

My first hour back in Manhattan
seemed to be more alive with fascinating detail and eccentricity than
my entire stay in Los Angeles. I walked the streets of the city with
ineffable joy, feeling like throwing a beret in the air à la Mary Tyler
Moore. I was actually shocked that in my absence New York had not
devolved into the nightmarish version depicted as Gotham City in
Batman. In Los Angeles, where condemning New York was a favorite
pastime, every pleasure there was referenced by a corresponding evil
in New York. It helped the many ex–New Yorkers justify living in a
city so diametrically different. It was also surprising to find that New

Yorkers, on the other hand, rarely mentioned L.A.—not out of snobbery, but because the city was self-referential and no such comparison was needed.

I hungrily took in the mélange of sights, sounds, and smells: the homeless, the vendors, the traffic, the many characters. I even enjoyed the cold February air. Every aspect of the city that had oppressed or disgusted me nine months before captivated me now. I paused at the corner of 44th Street and Broadway and smiled at the scene: A woman was peddling "disembodied" rubber hands that wriggled realistically on top of an overturned cardboard box, not far from a Senegali man selling faux Rolex watches and T-shirts that read DIE YUPPIE SCUM.

I had also become part of the trend of twenty-somethings to move back with their parents. Unlike many, however, I was received with open arms. My father, so relieved that I had returned from Los Angeles, was going out of his way to be nice to me, even lending me his car and stocking the refrigerator with my favorite foods. He unnervingly kept saying, "You've just got to get back on the track— back on the track." But I wondered where the track was heading and whether it was worth getting on at all.

When I moved back to New York, I reasoned that perhaps it was L.A. that was the problem. Perhaps, too, it was the atmosphere in the "majors" (the major film studios, recognized as Warner, Universal, Paramount, Disney, Columbia/Tri-Star, Fox, and MGM) that turned me off. What I needed to find was a funky independent film company that distributed quality films from New York.

My Left Foot. sex, lies and videotape. Cinema Paradiso. Wonderful films distributed by an independent film company in New York called Miramax Films. An independent that had thrived at a time when many others like DeLaurentiis Entertainment Group, Cannon, New World Pictures, Vestron, and Weintraub Entertainment had filed for bankruptcy. A company that had consistently brought quality films to the screen while Hollywood pandered to the core movie audience, young people aged twelve to twenty-nine. The coolest, hippest film company in the industry, according to the glowing press articles I had read. I wanted in.

Through Marcia Spano at CAA, I arranged an interview with John Schmidt, chief financial officer at Miramax. Brother of Benno Schmidt, then president of Yale, John was an MBA trying to professionalize a family-run company. He was friendly to me from the start of the interview. It seemed mutually beneficial. They needed an eager MBA to organize the accounting statements for *The Long Walk Home,* the Whoopi Goldberg film about the civil rights struggle and the Montgomery bus boycott of 1955. I needed a job in order to preserve my sanity while I searched for other positions. And, if it worked out, who knew? But talk about lower expectations—I was thrilled to be making the equivalent of $35,000 a year.

I started the job quite happily, even enjoying the tedious accounting work. This was nitty-gritty bookkeeping, with ledger accounts and piles of crumpled invoices. And I loved our small crew in the finance and accounting area. We were the nerds and suits, to be sure, but we were the nerds and suits in a hip and fast-paced art-house film company, which made all the difference in the world. We were also housed on the third floor of the Tribeca Film Center, a renovated, prewar, red-brick building in downtown Manhattan, which Robert DeNiro co-owned. I was excited about being back in the city and working around quality films every day.

I had heard much about the famed Weinstein brothers before going to work at Miramax. Raised in Flushing and sons of a 47th Street diamond cutter, they had gotten their start at the State University of New York at Buffalo where they were student rock promoters. They dropped out of college and purchased a movie theater in Buffalo where they presented rock and roll acts, as well as second- and third-run films. Their first major acquisition was in 1982, when they paid $180,000 for a five-hour tape of two benefit concerts for Amnesty International with performances by Sting, Eric Clapton, Monty Python, and Phil Collins. The Weinsteins edited the footage down to two hours, called the film *The Secret Policeman's Other Ball,* and distributed it throughout the United States. After the film became a cult hit and took in over $6 million at the box office, the brothers moved to Manhattan and formed Miramax, a company dedicated to distributing quality independent films. Their successful string of film acquisitions allowed them to cautiously expand to their present modern offices and forty-person staff.

Press articles had described them as looking like supermarket managers, used-car dealers, and loading dock workers. When I saw "the boys," two overweight, unkempt, and yes, grotesque-looking guys running through the office barking orders, I immediately knew who they were and realized that I was not going to be introduced to them. I did have a tough time telling which one was which, but quickly learned that thirty-six-year-old Bob, who oversaw business matters, was the one with gold-framed aviator glasses. And thirty-eight-year-old Harvey, who was more the creative head, was the fatter of the two, prone to chain-smoking and wearing baggy black turtlenecks, which made him all the more sweaty.

Looks are deceiving, we are often told. Sometimes, unpleasant appearances and bad manners mask people with big hearts. Thus, I wanted to judge these two characters on my own without influence from fellow employees. One indication that Miramax was not very different from the studio environment came when I dared to casually flip through a copy of *Daily Variety,* which was lying on a pile of mail on the secretary's desk outside of Harvey's office. His secretary rushed over, a terrified look on her face. "If Harvey walks out and sees you looking at his magazines before he sees them, he'll go nuts!"

The brothers' behavior was every bit as bad as advertised. In the columns Harvey wrote for *Premiere* magazine, he came across as articulate, witty, sensitive, and personable. He was none of the above with his staff, frequently dressing them down in the middle of the offices. Bob was no better, and the two thundered through the office, slamming doors and yelling and cursing at each other and at employees throughout the day.

I remember one day when we gathered to celebrate Harvey's birthday in the main conference room. The staffers gathered once or twice a month for the employee birthday ritual when we sang "Happy Birthday" and ate cake. The birthday was secondary, as the main objective was to escape from the grind of work for a few minutes and gossip with fellow Miramaxers. We waited expectantly that day for twenty minutes until Harvey shyly peeked his head into the room, having been conned into thinking that this was a production meeting. He stayed for all of three minutes, making little eye contact with anyone; it was apparent to us that it was difficult for him to be in such close proximity to all the employees at one time. That was too personal, and he couldn't handle it.

Given the brothers' behavior, it was all the more incongruous to meet their sweet Jewish mother, Miriam, who still regarded the two as her darling little babies. The matriarch and namesake of the firm (Miramax was named for the brothers' parents, Miriam and Max) visited the office on various occasions, particularly on Jewish holidays, walking through the office with a tray of pastries and candies for the nice boys and girls working for her sons.

Funny place, Miramax. Outside of fast-food chains, I've never seen a business with such high turnover. Between the constant firings and resignations, the average employee's tenure was six months or less. The Weinstein brothers didn't seem to care when their junior people left. As long as Bob and Harvey were there, it seemed acceptable to them to serve as an industry training ground. By the time I had been there three months, I felt like a veteran and I was, as a glance at the employee phone list (updated weekly) confirmed. In fact, I learned that there was a support group of sorts in L.A. for former Miramax employees, called Mir-Anon.

And contrary to New York City labor laws, there was no minimum wage at Miramax. It was a simple matter of supply and demand; the minimum was what the marketplace was willing to bear, and many hopefuls were eager to work for free. Thus, every executive, no matter how young or junior, had a stable of twenty-something interns, eagerly doing grunt work gratis.

As for the finance and accounting department, we were left in the dark by the creative staff and treated like moldy mushrooms. Even the controller, a lovable nerd named Irwin, could not talk directly with Bob and Harvey without going through the chief financial officer. It was the accounting staff, however, who had to take the heat from irate producers and other profit participants who were being paid at the last possible moment, and who inevitably sent auditing teams to check Miramax's books in order to ascertain whether or not they were being cheated. It seemed like few who had business dealings with the brothers trusted them to deal ethically with them.

I studied many of the film contracts and found that the basic arithmetic of film financing made it difficult for distributors to show big profits on their books. It was these elusive profits which Art Buchwald tried to find in his case against Paramount. An independent film company, like Miramax, purchased the distribution rights to a film. Whatever the gross, approximately half went to theater owners. Miramax then took a 30 to 35 percent distribution fee, various gross participations were taken out, and the costs of prints, publicity, advertising, and interest were deducted. After the producers had recouped the costs of production and various net participants had taken their share, only then was the film able to show profits. These profits were distributed per contract to various parties on a pro rata basis. A rule of thumb was that a picture had to gross approximately two and a half to three times its cost just for the distributor to break even. It had to make considerably more for others to share in profits. That was why ancillary markets, such as foreign distribution, home video, cable, and network television, were so critical to a film's profitability.

The one event that brought all departments together was the film premieres. We were all invited to attend the opening of Miramax's films, as well as the premiere party afterwards with the cast. It was the perfect opportunity for me to impress a date by showing her I was a big shot in the industry. Once again, though, even in a tiny company, the dichotomy between the creative and business sides was painfully apparent at these premieres. You would never know from watching the two groups socializing in separate cliques that they worked for the same firm (I doubt Harvey could have picked out more than half of his employees from the crowd). Still, it was our only perk, akin to the discount Will Keller received at Disneyland.

Say what you wanted about the brothers, they had terrific taste in film. They located and acquired films that catered to all that was noble and intelligent in the filmgoing audience. Like few others in the industry, they appealed to the highest common denominator. You could hardly blame them then for doing whatever had to be done to promote a film. They learned very early on that controversy and strong emotions often yielded free press coverage, which in turn boosted a film's box office. That's why they distributed *The Cook, the Thief, His Wife and Her Lover,* Madonna's *Truth or Dare,* and the X-rated *Tie Me Up! Tie Me Down!,* films other distributors lacked the courage to distribute.

I was surprised, however, at how far the brothers would go in their promotion activities. One day, I saw a well-dressed black woman talking with Bob and Harvey. In a company without a single minority in the professional ranks (other than their manager of computer systems), this was definitely newsworthy. I went to the office gossip wags (for a small company, Miramax had a powerful undercurrent of gossip) who informed me the woman was a recently hired MBA who was to undertake special projects for the brothers. A cynic would have pointed to the company's upcoming film, *A Rage in Harlem,* and remarked that this film had influenced their hiring. The cynic would have watched how the Weinsteins directed this woman to organize a well-publicized film premiere in Harlem's Apollo theater and might have concluded that they used her to show off their progressiveness and to deflect any criticism aimed at them. Anyone would have become skeptical after the Weinsteins fired this woman shortly after the film had finished its run.

During my four months at Miramax, I learned from Harvey and Bob that it doesn't matter how much of an asshole you are to your employees. As long as you produce quality films and make good money, you're the darling of the press and a hero in the industry. As one producer remarked in *New York* magazine, "They lie and they try to screw you, but in the end, they care about the movie."

Harvey and Bob readily admit to their poor work habits, even to the point of glorifying these attributes. In a playful letter to the *Los Angeles Times,* the boys wrote:

> We just wanted to let you know that we have signed up for a series of Management 101 courses at a local community college. Our day now consists of:
>
> 9 A.M.: How to Get Rid of Our Type-A Personalities.
> 10 A.M.: How to Delegate Authority.
> 11 A.M.: Dealing With Your Current Employees.
> Noon–5 P.M.: Dealing With Your Ex-Employees.
> 5–5:15 P.M.: Brotherly Love, Meditation & Chanting.
> 5:15–6 P.M.: Corporatespeak.

The company's turnover continued after I left. John Schmidt quit and joined competitor October Films, and later told the *New York Times*: "I left Miramax because my mother and father were not named Miriam and Max. It's completely a family operation and ultimately they look only to each other at the end of the day."

Miramax, however, continued to prosper, and each year, it seemed, the Weinsteins were able to harvest the best of the independent film crop before the pictures even got to film festivals like

Cannes or Sundance. In 1992, they made another savvy purchase with *The Crying Game*. They paid $4 million for United States theatrical rights and mounted a clever ad campaign ("Don't tell the secret"). The film grossed over $60 million in the U.S. and garnered six Academy Award nominations, winning for Best Original Screenplay. Flush with this success, the Weinsteins were able to sell Miramax for a reported $65 million to Walt Disney Studios, and to continue to operate somewhat autonomously within Disney. Once again, the Weinsteins were rewarded for their great taste in film and their knack for trusting their own instincts. In 1993, they continued their streak with *The Piano*, which won three Oscars. And in 1994, they released *Pulp Fiction*, the Quentin Tarantino film they financed and produced, which won the Palme d'Or at Cannes and received seven Academy Award nominations.

The business press continued to heap accolades on the brothers. *Fortune* magazine was astute enough, however, to add the Weinsteins to their annual list of the toughest (read, meanest) bosses in America.

CHAPTER 16

No Regrets

We shall not cease from exploration
And the end of all our exploring
Will be to arrive where we started
And know the place for the first time.

T.S. ELIOT

I don't like work—no man does—but what I like is
in the work—the chance to find yourself.

JOSEPH CONRAD

The Miramax experience was the final blow, convincing me that the fundamentals of the movie industry were the same, whether in L.A. or New York. The fire that once burned in me to make it in Hollywood at all costs had finally been extinguished. Without second-guessing myself, I could leave the film industry behind and get on with my life.

Though I had gotten offers to work as assistant to various executives, I was unwilling to join the ranks of the young wannabes, working under duress for the industry's power brokers, waiting in desperation for their time to come. I had seen enough of the underbelly of Hollywood—the thousands of people on the fringes, a few of whom would become the next generation of executives, most of whom would always be on the sidelines watching and envying the handful of executives who were at the top of the industry. In an article in *Variety* entitled "How Hollywood Eats Its Young," various creative executive hopefuls described their plight in dour terms. "For most of us," one twenty-six-year-old said, "it's like walking down a dark hallway where you can't see where you are or where you're going, and you can't feel the walls."

But I'm not some Generation X–er who's afraid of work. I can deal perfectly well with short-term sacrifice in pursuit of a larger goal. It was the realization that this prize was not worth winning that stopped me in my tracks. I no longer desired the positions of the senior creative executives for whom I'd be working.

I moved to L.A. straight out of business school for the chance to be associated with new film projects. But of all the thousands of scripts that landed in Hollywood each year, a mere fifteen to twenty on average were made into films by each studio. This meant that the creative executives spent most of their time saying no and the rest fighting for their jobs. Deep down they knew that they couldn't accurately predict successful films and that, given the chance, many others could perform equally well. This impostor complex seemed to be rampant among the ranks of production executives.

Anyone reading the executive changes each day in *Variety* would notice that executives took full credit for all the profitable pictures produced during their stint at the studio, no matter how insignificant the role they played in its production. Meanwhile, no one seemed to have worked on the many flops. This was, after all, an industry whose most famous maxim was screenwriter William Goldman's pronouncement that "nobody knows anything." It was invoked ad nauseam to explain surprise hits or bombs. A senior producer explained the science of moviemaking in *New York* magazine: "I honestly believe the Movie God flies around this town and settles down at a commissary for a couple of years and then flies on."

And, my epiphany notwithstanding, neither was my love of film justification in itself for pursuing this industry. *Everyone* loves the movies. Movies, to be sure, are fun, joyous, and sometimes meaningful. But the movie business and its executives did not seem very fun or joyous. The product was surely distinct from the process. I couldn't help but feel that the chipmunks and mice plastered on all the wooden signs on the Disney lot were the only characters there with genuine smiles.

Most creative executives I met were neither creative nor geniuses. They were, however, burning with raw hunger and would rip your heart out if it would help get them ahead. They were what my father called "killers," and this quality more than made up for their deficiencies.

David Geffen, who worked his way up from the mailroom of the William Morris Agency to a $1 billion fortune, was the ultimate embodiment of success in Hollywood. And yet, he openly acknowledged that as a college dropout, he had lied to get the William Morris job by claiming to have graduated from UCLA (he hadn't even gotten into UCLA, instead attending and flunking out of both the University of Texas at Austin and Brooklyn College). Once in the mailroom, he intercepted the letter from the university that denied he had gotten a degree, and inserted a forged letter that attested to his graduation. Years later, his fame and fortune undeniable, this tale was pointed to as a symbol of his street smarts and ingenuity. "I just don't believe in taking no for an answer," he said confidently in magazine profiles.

Of course I'd like to be one of the handful of top executives in Hollywood, like Geffen or Ovitz, whose support can make a project happen. But what pact did one have to make with the devil to get there? There was a cost to this success. I had seen the price up close in the unhappy faces of the power executives who routinely worked eighty-hour weeks and whose social lives were inseparable from their work world.

I was fearful of continuing in this industry because I admired and respected so few of the film executives I met. These executives were average, normal people on their own. But doing well in the industry and being a nice guy did not seem to go hand in hand. The industry espoused egomania and greed that would have disgraced executives in other industries but was rewarded in Hollywood.

I don't know how this story ends. The denouement is still unclear. I have settled back into some semblance of routine. I live in my home city, work in my original profession, and do many of the same activities I did before business school. A rational person (most likely in the voice of my father) might easily ask, "So Ev, what was the point?"

My father's voice, as usual, is both aggravating and illuminating. What was the point of a career move that decimated my ego, cut my salary to near minimum wage and, ultimately, landed me almost exactly where I began? A spiritual journey that ended with a painful epiphany in a Jack in the Box? A search for clarity, purpose, and meaning that drove me to employ the services of a 1-900-TAROT reader? How do I explain this "vision quest" to others and, most importantly, to myself?

Sitting in my cubicle in a climate-controlled bank of offices in a skyscraper in midtown Manhattan, doing work I would have once considered far too boring for a would-be producer, I have the strangest feeling. Dare I call it contentment? As harebrained and looney as my Hollywood detour might seem to my parents and friends, there is a wonderful feeling about having given it a shot. About never torturing myself with "what ifs" and "might have beens." So I never became a hot-shot producer. I didn't become a Brad Dorman either. I didn't learn to stomp on my assistants, lie, cheat, and humiliate people. I would never measure my self-worth by how many phone calls I *didn't* return each day. Nor would I ever ruin my physical and mental health by making horrible movies like *Out on a Limb*. And I learned that even if you (and your brother) have the best taste in movies on the planet, you can still be a repulsive human being.

So that's it? I wasted a year of my life to discover that Hollywood's magic kingdom was run by witches, wolves, and evil trolls? Okay, I could have read that in a hundred books. I could have rented *The Day of the Locust* or *The Player* or *Barton Fink*, but I had to go find out for myself.

Go ahead...Call me an idiot...Call me a *schmuck*. Just don't call me a *wannabe* anymore.

AFTERWORD

"Look for the ridiculous in everything and you find it."

JULES RENARD

In the two years since *Wannabe* was first published, I've often felt that the book was incomplete. Many of the bizarre events that occurred after its publication seemed worthy of inclusion. The story needed a coda, if only to demystify the experience of being published.

At first the attention was intoxicating: book signings, interviews, photo sessions, and talk-show appearances. And then, without warning, the moment was up and the wolf pack moved on. I was left rereading the articles, watching myself gush on TV, and wondering if the image of myself refracted in the media's house of mirrors was close to what I had envisioned when I first fantasized about getting my manuscript published. I knew that publicity was vital to entice the fickle reader. But in the columnists' hands, *Wannabe* became yet another gossip book, just a meatier version of the *National Enquirer*. "Hot and Juicy Dishes from a Hollywood 'Wannabe,'" promised *USA Today*. "H'wood tell-all," chimed the *New York Post*.

Still, I dutifully performed like a trained seal. I found myself seated on the pastel stage of the "Sally Jesse Raphael Show" for the taping of her Summer Gossip Special. Joining me were four highly unlikely copanelists: Rose Kennedy's former personal assistant, who had recently penned her memoirs; Mr. Blackwell, the self-proclaimed arbiter of women's fashion, who was promoting his autobiography, *From Rags to Bitches*; Lady Colin Campbell, a royal watcher there to discuss her tell-all on Princess Diana; and a journalist who had written a biography of Marcia Clark.

With ten minutes to go in the hour-long show, I was sure I was going to be bumped. Then Sally looked at one of the cameras and adjusted her trademark oversized red glasses. "Coming up next, this wannabe says it was his big dream to go to Hollywood and have his name in lights. You won't believe what happened when he got there. Stay with us." While we waited for a commercial break, I looked out at the crowd of middle-aged housewives and wondered again why my publisher believed this to be our target audience.

The jazzy theme music played and the audience applauded on cue. Sally asked me why I left Wall Street to pursue Hollywood. I cited my love of film and explained that my goal was not to be an actor but a production executive. All hopes of conducting a mature discussion were then dashed.

"I don't know how he made it," said Mr. Blackwell, "but he should have learned from me. I made it on the casting couch!"

Sally smelled a TV moment and pounced: "Everett, did anyone ever ask you to go on the casting couch?"

"No, I think that exists, but—"

"Stand up and let us see!" hammed Mr. Blackwell, a tanned gray-haired man with a gold ring in his left earlobe.

I laughed with the audience, held up my hands, and took the high road. "This show is taking a direction I don't want to follow." But I was learning the art of self-promotion, and I rushed to tell my Alec Baldwin and Leonard Nimoy anecdotes before they flashed the closing credits and promotional ads for Chap Stick, Compound W, and Jenny Craig.

Radio interviews are even lower on the publicity food chain. Mine were indistinguishable, whether I was featured on the morning commute program in Topeka, Seattle, or Buffalo. A three-minute spot with a hollering, bell-ringing "morning zoo crew" urging me to give up some dirt, hoping I'd seen Kim Basinger naked or better yet, slept with her. Rare was the disk jockey who had even read the inside cover. "Hey campers (ding, ding), if you want the scoop on Hollywood, we've got on the phone with us now Everett Weinberger from New York. HELLO Mr. WANNABE! Wannabe, wannabe, wannabe! (Ding, ding, ding.)" Sitting at my work cubicle, hoping no one could hear me, I wondered what the chances were of even one person listening during his seven A.M. commute who would be so inspired that he'd swerve into the nearest Barnes & Noble.

While the publication hoopla was often less than satisfying, I never tired of hearing the heartfelt stories from fellow wannabes who phoned or wrote me. Some had recently finished their own harrowing stints in the entertainment business; others were considering similar migrations from their hometowns to Los Angeles. Several said I had depressed them, discouraging them from investigating the industry any further. I tried to convince them that rather than accepting my stories as gospel, they ought to pursue their dreams and find out the truth for themselves.

After the *People* magazine review appeared, however, I began receiving a different sort of communiqué from women who had seen my photo in the article and had no intention of reading the book. They had more primordial needs in mind.

My introduction to this market segment came via a manila envelope addressed to me in childlike block letters. Inside were color brochures depicting Napa Valley wineries and hot air balloons, a photo of a stocky, fierce-looking young woman standing in front of a lake somewhere in Northern California, and a sheet of loose-leaf paper crammed with neatly written words. The woman introduced herself and described her tastes in great detail, from alcoholic beverages (Singapore Slings and daiquiris) to home furnishings (contemporary furniture and artwork). She made it clear that she was looking for a man like me and if it was reciprocal, I should phone her. She twice indicated that if I wasn't interested, I was to return her "original photo." I shook my head and put the letter aside.

A week later I was watching television in my apartment when the phone rang. No one seemed to be on the other line. And then, a soft and tentative hello. "Uh, this is Cathy," she said in a deep voice. "Did you get my letter and photo?"

Seconds passed before I comprehended. Recent stalker headlines flashed in my mind. Nervously, I thanked her, hastily ad-libbing that I was seeing someone. "Well then can you send me my original photo back?" I ran out to the corner mailbox that night.

Not all the feedback was so positive. A few of the people mentioned in the book contacted me to voice their displeasure at seeing their names in print. So it was with lawsuits in mind that I returned a call from Mark Bove, director of development at David Kirkpatrick's Event Movie Company.

"David loved *Wannabe* and wanted to know if movie rights are available."

I asked Bove to repeat that. "Are you sure he read the book, especially the chapter about him?"

He laughed. "Yes, of course. He was actually flattered to be a mythical, bad-guy character. David liked it in a weird, perverted way."

I assured him that the book had not been optioned and advised him to call my agent (after all, Kirkpatrick was still a minor player, producing such films as *The Brady Bunch Movie* and *The Evening Star*). But after several conference calls, an offer was never extended, which left me wondering whether the exercise had been nothing more than a sly attempt by Kirkpatrick to take the property off the market permanently. I learned later, though, that Kirkpatrick had been genuinely interested but had second thoughts regarding how he'd come off in a filmed version. (I also discovered to my amusement that Brad Dorman, initially promoted to director of development, had eventually been fired by Kirkpatrick and subsequently left the industry—to become a stockbroker.)

I was eventually wooed by another Hollywood hitter, David Brown, the mustached octogenarian uber-producer of such films as *Jaws, The Verdict, A Few Good Men*, and most importantly, *The Player* (and better known as the husband of Helen Gurley Brown). Brown acquired a one-year option to produce either a movie or television series based on the book. Though I was anxious to meet him and find out what plans he had for *Wannabe: The Film*, four months passed before I was able to land on his schedule.

We met for lunch in a midtown Manhattan Japanese restaurant. While he recalled his halcyon days working for Darryl F. Zanuck at Twentieth–Century Fox, my fingers battled with chopsticks guiding chunks of raw salmon to my lips. I was rapt as he alternately praised *Wannabe* and decried the deteriorating state of affairs in Hollywood for newcomers. Both Brown and his director of development, Kit Golden, seemed eager to demonstrate that they were different from the slimier characters mentioned in *Wannabe*. They needn't have worried, as I liked them, wishing I had known them back when.

But I'm not going to tell you that this story ends with a multi-million dollar film deal—although it was fun hearing Brown hypothesize on which A-list actors could play me. (Alec Baldwin? Perfect!) The following letter arrived eight months later on letterhead from The Manhattan Project, Brown's production company.

Dear Everett,

It is with great sadness that I must report our failure to set your wonderful book *Wannabe* up for movie or television development. There are some production reasons for this—new sets for every episode, for example—and ironically the fact that my own film *The Player* has been acquired for a possible series. I told your agent to let some younger turk run with it and prove me a dunce. Good luck and thanks for the opportunity.

Warm regards,
David Brown

I've come a long way in seven years. I now have my very own project in turnaround!

September 1997
New York, New York